Low-Temperature Precision Cooking

Modern Techniques for Perfect Cooking Through Science,
Ultimate Low-Temperature Immersion Circulator Guide

Sarah P. Williamson

Low-Temperature Precision Cooking: Modern Techniques for Perfect Cooking Through Science, Ultimate Low-Temperature Immersion Circulator Guide

Table of Contents

Book 1 - Sous Vide

Modern Techniques for Perfect Cooking Through Science (Scrumptious Dinners, Gourmet Cookbook, Precision Cooking)

1 - Introduction

Benefits of Cooking the Sous Vide Way

Sous vide sounds too fancy to apply to cooking, but it simply means placing your ingredients in a container (a cooking pouch or canning jar can be used) and then dropping the container into a heated water bath set at a target temperature. As soon as your food reaches the intended time or temperature, you remove it from the water bath, finish (for example, by giving it a quick sear) it, and enjoy it.

Everything Tastes Better

Cooking the sous vide way gives you food that simply tastes way better than if you cooked it using conventional methods. Your tenderloin steaks turn out juicier and perfectly done around the edges, your beef or lamb ribs almost melt as they touch your mouth, your fish fillets are succulent and their centers are as evenly cooked as their edges.

Even an egg can be cooked the sous vide way, and you will be amazed at how delicate and custard-like your poached egg turns out.

Carved in History

Since the ancient times, the practice of preserving and cooking different kinds of food in sealed containers or packages has been around. Culinary history records will tell you that people have been wrapping food in leaves, sealing them inside the bladders of animals, packing them in salt, or potting them in fat prior to cooking.

They already had the idea that preventing food from being exposed to air can slow down its decay - something that vacuum sealing successfully does. As a bonus, packaging your food also helps keep it succulent, not dried out.

Precision, Perfection

"Sous vide" is a French term that means "under vacuum." The sous vide cooking method does utilize vacuum sealing food, but its important feature is precise temperature control. Cooking your food the sous vide way means you use a heater that is computer-controlled to bring a water bath to the target temperature and then keep the water bath at that temperature for hours or days.

Having the ability to control temperature or heat in cooking your food gives you the freedom to go about the cooking process without being a slave to time.

When using the conventional oven or grill, you have to deal with extreme temperatures as well as fluctuating temperatures – this is why it is important to get your exact cooking times straight, since going a little off the mark results in foods that do not turn out as they should.

But if you cook using the sous vide method, your foods are guaranteed to taste just right, giving you ample time to focus on the other aspects of food preparation.

But First, Safety

The sous vide way of cooking's use of accurate and uniform temperatures provide you other benefits:

Your food turn out evenly cooked through, so you can say goodbye to rare centers and overly dried-out edges; you get the same perfectly cooked results every single time you cook; and most importantly, you can rest assured that any potential pathogens in your food, especially in chicken and other poultry meats, are killed for your safety.

Have It All

Lastly, cooking your food in a closed container allows you to provide a completely humid environment for your ingredients. This is what braises your food in an effective manner and gives you markedly more scrumptious and more succulent results.

Simply searing your sous vide cooked food (which do not brown) will give them those traditional flavors you have gotten used to, so you actually get to enjoy both the nostalgic taste of your old style cooking and the gourmet flavors imparted by the scientific sous vide method.

Tips and Tricks for Sous Vide Cooking

Digging into gourmet quality dishes does not have to be tricky. Simplify sous vide cooking by following these tips:

Pouching

Prepping your food for sous vide cooking is as easy as buy, portion, and seal:

1. Purchase economy size packages of chicken, fish, and steak.

2. Divide your meats and other proteins into individual servings, then place each serving into individual cooking pouches.

3. Don't forget to include your favorite seasonings before vacuum sealing the cooking pouch.

2 - Saving Time on Cooking

Cutting down on your cooking time has never been easier:

Cook, then freeze

- Season your food and place in the cooking pouches.

- Vacuum seal and place in the sous vide water oven to cook.

- Place the cooking pouches in an ice bath for thirty to forty-five minutes.

- Label the pouches with date and contents.

- Place in the freezer (use within a year).

- Take the pouch out of the freezer and thaw.

- Reheat for forty-five minutes for every inch of thickness.

- When reheating from frozen, reheat for thirty minutes more.

- Sear the reheated food and serve immediately with or without sauce.

Freeze, then cook

- Season your individual servings of fish, seafood, poultry, meat, or game.

- Place in the cooking pouches and vacuum seal.

- Write the date and contents on the label.

- Freeze the pouches with uncooked ingredients for no more than six weeks.

- Remove the pouches from the freezer and allow to thaw.

- Place in the sous vide water oven to cook at the target temperature.

- If cooking from frozen, cook for an additional thirty minutes.

- Serve sauced or seared.

Marinating

Marinate your foods with sous vide ease:

1. Place your fish/ meat/ poultry, vegetables, and other

ingredients in the cooking pouch. Add the marinade and then press with your hands (to remove air pockets) before sealing manually.

2. Place the cooking pouch in the freezer to allow the marinade to set.

3. Take the pouch out of the freezer and cut through the pouch (below the seal).

4. Vacuum seal the pouch and submerge in the sous vide water oven (preheated to target temperature). If cooking from frozen, allow to cook for an additional thirty minutes.

3 - Cooking Efficiently

Group similar food to save time:

Cooking vegetables

You can cook most vegetables in the temperature range of 183 degrees Fahrenheit to 185 degrees Fahrenheit. The food will generally become tender within forty-five minutes to one hour in the sous vide water oven.

To save time, you can submerge several cooking pouches containing different types of vegetables in the sous vide water oven all at once. You can then consume the cooked vegetables for several days. This trick may have you spending some hands-on veggie prepping time.

It does allow you to literally just leave them to cook on their own. While your sous vide water oven is cooking all the vegetables you need for the next three days, you can work on your exercise routine, play with your baby, or watch your favorite TV reruns.

Cooking meats

You can cook meats (beef, duck, lamb, ostrich, bison, and other red meats – placed inside different cooking pouches) at the same time and at the same sous vide water oven temperature of 134 degrees Fahrenheit (for that perfectly medium-rare doneness). Just keep in mind that the length of cooking time will vary, depending on the toughness as well as the thickness of the meat cut.

If you would rather have your meat cooked medium or well-done, simply set your sous vide water oven to 140 degrees or 150 degrees Fahrenheit. Any which way, you can rest assured that your meat will be cooked evenly from the center to the edges.

After seasoning your meats, portion them according to your needs and then place inside their cooking pouches. Vacuum seal before cooking all at once in the sous vide water oven at their target temperature.

Once cooked, remove the pouches from the sous vide water oven and place in an ice bath. Dry off the pouches before labeling with their respective dates and contents, then place in the refrigerator to chill for up to two days, or place in the freezer to keep for up to one year.

Cooking tougher meat cuts

Tougher meat cuts include spare ribs, roasts, and grass-fed

beef. Simply tenderize overnight by cooking for 8 to 10 hours or more.

Cooking poultry

You can cook chicken meat (or turkey) along with pork at the temperature range of 140 degrees Fahrenheit to 146 degrees Fahrenheit for two hours to two hours and thirty minutes. Submerge up to 12 chicken breasts, or 8 turkey breasts, or 6 pork tenderloins, or 16 pork chops, or any combination of these meats.

As soon as they are cooked, remove from the sous vide water oven and their cooking pouches, then submerge in an ice bath. Dry off and label before refrigerating for up to two days or freezing up to one year.

Reheating previously cooked food

While your fish is cooking in the sous vide water oven, you can add in pouches containing cooked veggies to reheat them. A ½-inch fish fillet's delicate flesh only requires 20 to 40 minutes of cooking, so you can drop and reheat one to two pouches of cooked veggies in the sous vide water oven as the fish cooks.

Doing it this way allows you to have delicious, nutritious, and effortless dinner ready within just 30 to 40 minutes.

Multitask cooking

As long as there is enough space in the sous vide water oven, you can cook pork spare ribs for thirty hours at 176 degrees along with chicken, turkey, or duck leg quarters (which also cook at the same target temperature).

4 - Succulent Sous Vide Fish for Dinner Recipes

Dill Caper and Artichoke Salmon

Ingredients:

Salmon:

- Kosher salt (1/2 cup)

- Dill, fresh, chopped (1 teaspoon)

- Liquid smoke, Applewood (1 tablespoon)

- Salmon steaks, boned removed, 2" (4 pieces)

- Brown sugar (1/2 cup)

- Pepper, freshly ground (1/2 teaspoon)

- Olive oil, extra virgin (2 tablespoons)

Artichokes:

- Lemon juice, freshly squeezed (1/2 tablespoon)

- Artichokes, trimmed, w/choke removed (4 pieces)

- Salt (1/4 teaspoon)

- Pepper, freshly ground (1/4 teaspoon)

Sauce:

- Butter, melted (4 ounces)

- Dill, fresh, chopped (1 tablespoon)

- Dijon mustard (1/2 teaspoon)

- Egg yolks (3 pieces)

- Capers, chopped (1 tablespoon)

- Salt (1/2 teaspoon + ¼ teaspoon)

- Lemon juice, freshly squeezed (1 tablespoon + ½ tablespoon)

Directions:

1. Place the pepper, sugar, and dill in a medium bowl. Add the salt and liquid smoke. Stir to combine into a paste. Rub all surfaces of the salmon steaks with the paste, making sure they are evenly covered. Place the salmon steaks on a large plate, then wrap with cling film before placing in the refrigerator for one hour.

2. Rinse the steaks thoroughly until all traces of the paste are gone. Use paper towels to pat dry afterwards. Working in batches, place the steaks inside cooking pouches. Vacuum seal the pouches before placing in the refrigerator until cooking time.

3. Fill the sous vide water oven and then preheat to 185 degrees.

4. Meanwhile, trim and peel the artichoke stems before rubbing with lemon juice. Place in a cooking pouch, vacuum seal, and submerge in the sous vide water oven. Cook for about one hour and fifteen minutes or until tenderly cooked. Transfer the pouch containing the artichokes onto a plate before lowering the sous vide water oven's temperature to 149 degrees.

5. Fill a cooking pouch with the ingredients for the sauce. Vacuum seal before submerging in the sous vide water oven to cook for forty-five minutes. Once done, transfer to a blender filled with capers and dill. Process until well-emulsified and thick, pour into a cooking pouch, and vacuum seal. Place in the sous vide water oven again to keep warm (do the same to

the cooked artichokes).

6. Lower the sous vide water oven temperature further to 134 degrees. Drop the pouch containing the chilled salmon steaks and allow to cook for one hour along with the artichokes and sauce.

7. In the meantime, heat a well-greased grill until extremely hot.

8. Once the salmon steaks are done. Then remove from the water oven and set on a tray. Do the same with the artichokes.

9. Brush a bit of olive oil on all sides of the salmon steaks and artichokes, then sprinkle pepper and salt on the artichokes alone. Place the salmon steaks on the grill and cook for thirty seconds on each side or until seared and golden; repeat with the artichokes. Once done, transfer onto a serving platter (warmed), making sure the artichokes surround the salmon.

10. Take the sauce out of the sous vide water oven and pour on top of the salmon steaks and artichokes. Serve right away.

Easy and Delicious Salmon

Ingredients:

- Kosher salt (1 ½ teaspoons)

- Butter, unsalted, sliced into 4 portions (28 grams)

- King salmon, skinless, boneless, 6 ounces (4 pieces)

- Lemon slices, fresh (4 pieces)

Directions:

1. Fill the sous vide water oven before preheating to 126 degrees.

2. Meanwhile, sprinkle salt on the salmon pieces before topping each with a slice of lemon and a portion of butter.

3. Transfer 2 salmon portions into a cooking pouch. Vacuum seal the two pouches before submerging in the sous vide water oven. Cook for twenty minutes.

4. Meanwhile, heat a skillet before adding a little oil.

5. Once the salmon is done, remove from the sous vide

water and transfer onto the hot, greased skillet. Cook for one to two minutes or until the salmon pieces are caramelized on the surface.

6. Serve and enjoy.

Yummy Cranberry Salmon

Ingredients:

- Cilantro, fresh, chopped (a handful)

- Salmon fillets, boneless, skinless, 5 ounces (2 pieces)

- Marinade:

- Barbecue sauce (2 tablespoons)

- Cranberry juice (1 tablespoon)

- Salt (1/8 teaspoon)

- Cranberry sauce (2 tablespoons)

- Olive oil, extra virgin (1 tablespoon)

- Lime juice, freshly squeezed (1 teaspoon)

Directions:

1. Place all the ingredients for the marinade in a medium bowl. Stir to combine. Set aside 1½ tablespoons
   of the mixture for using later in a separate step.

2. Place the salmon fillets in the marinade and coat with
   the mixture on all sides. Cover the bowl before placing in the refrigerator for one to two hours.

3. Meanwhile, fill the sous vide water oven before preheating to 140 degrees.

4. Take the marinated salmon fillets out of the refrigerator and transfer into a cooking pouch. Vacuum seal,
   place in the sous vide water oven and cook for
   twenty-five to thirty minutes.

5. Set the broiler on high to preheat.

6. Once the salmon fillets are done. Then transfer to a
   pan (broiler-safe). Coat with the marinade you set
   aside earlier before placing in the broiler. Cook for
   one to two minutes or until heated through.

7. Top with chopped cilantro and serve immediately.
   Enjoy.

Chili Maple and Lemon Salmon

Ingredients:

- Sea salt, spiced (1 ½ tablespoons)

- Parsley, curly, freshly chopped (4 tablespoons)

- Maple syrup (4 ounces)

- Leeks, chopped (1 2/3 cups)

- Lemon zest, finely grated (1 tablespoon)

- Salmon fillet, fresh, scaled, 2 ½-oz. (4 pieces)

- Castor sugar (1 ½ tablespoons)

- Double cream (3 tablespoons + 1 teaspoon)

- Red chili, small (1 piece)

- Lemons, halved, caramelized (2 pieces)

Directions:

1. Mix the sugar and salt together before sprinkling on the fish fillets. Place the seasoned fillets in a large bowl, cover, and refrigerate for two hours.

2. Meanwhile, fill the sous vide water oven before pre-heating to 115 degrees.

3. Take the chilled fish fillets out of the refrigerator and lightly rinse before patting dry with paper towels and placing inside cooking pouches. After vacuum sealing the pouches, submerge in the preheated sous vide water oven. Allow the fish fillets to cook for forty-five minutes.

4. In the meantime, heat a water-filled pan on high. Allow the water to boil before adding the chopped leeks and salt. Boil for another two to three minutes, then drain and rinse with cold water. Drain again before squeezing the leeks until thoroughly dry. Place in a small bowl and set aside.

5. Heat another pan on medium. Add the cream and allow to boil to slightly thicken it. Stir in the leeks and cook for one to two minutes or until warmed through. Stir in the black pepper and salt. Then reduce heat to low to keep the mixture warm.

6. Heat another saucepan (small) on medium after pouring in the maple syrup. Once the syrup is cara-

melized, cover the pan and set aside to keep warm.

7. Slice the chili into lengthwise halves before removing the stems and deseeding. Mince the flesh and stir into the maple syrup. Stir in the lemon zest, black pepper, and chopped parsley as well.

8. After taking the cooked salmon out of the sous vide water bath, pat dry with paper towels and brush with the maple syrup mixture.

9. Meanwhile, pour the leek mixture onto a platter. Add the salmon on top.

10. Serve drizzled with more maple syrup mixture and enjoy.

Italian Style Poached Cod

Ingredients:

Cod:

- Olive oil, extra virgin (3 tablespoons)

- Lemon zest (1/2 tablespoon)

- Cod fillets, skinless, 6-oz. (2 pieces)

- Parsley sprigs, fresh (2 pieces)

- Peppers & olives:

- Red peppers, roasted, chopped (1/3 cup)

- Black olives, sliced (1/3 cup)

- Salt, kosher (1/4 teaspoon)

- Pepper, freshly cracked (1/4 teaspoon)

- Onion, small, peeled, diced (1 piece)

- Rosemary, fresh, chopped finely (1 teaspoon)

- Red pepper flakes (a pinch)

Salsa:

- Garlic clove, peeled, crushed (1 piece)

- Balsamic vinegar (1 teaspoon)

- Salt, kosher (1/4 teaspoon)

- Pepper, freshly cracked (1/4 teaspoon)

- Plum tomatoes, sliced (1 ¼ cups)

- Olive oil, extra virgin (1 teaspoon)

- Paprika, smoked (1/4 teaspoon)

Directions:

1. Fill the sous vide water oven before preheating to 181 degrees.

2. Fill a cooking pouch (small) with the tomatoes. Add the olive oil and garlic, then vacuum seal and place in the sous vide water oven. Cook for forty-five minutes before transferring into the blender. Add the smoked paprika and vinegar, then process until well-blended and smooth. Season with pepper and salt before setting aside.

3. Lower the sous vide water oven's temperature to 132 degrees.

4. Heat a skillet on medium-high before adding olive oil. Stir in the diced onions and cook for three minutes or until translucent and fragrant. Add the red pepper, olives, and rosemary; stir to combine

with the onions. Reduce heat to medium and cook for an additional four to six minutes before sprinkling salt and pepper into the mixture. Remove from heat and set aside.

5. Place the fish inside a cooking pouch (large). Add the salt, pepper, and olive oil before vacuum sealing the pouch. Submerge into the sous vide water oven to cook for twenty minutes.

6. Meanwhile, pour the tomato mixture onto a plate. Once the fish is cooked, place on top of the tomato mixture. Pour the onions and olives over the fish before garnishing with fresh parsley.

7. Serve sprinkled with lemon zest.

5 - Evenly Tender Sous Vide Poultry for Dinner Recipes

Paleo Friendly Crispy Chicken

Ingredients:

- Butter, unsalted (6 tablespoons)

- Black pepper, freshly ground (1/2 teaspoon)

- Garlic powder (1/4 teaspoon)

- Thyme, dried (1/4 teaspoon)

- Kosher salt (1/4 teaspoon)

- Lard (2 tablespoons)

- Chicken thighs, boneless, skin-on (6 pieces)

Directions:

1. Fill the sous vide water oven before preheating to 150 degrees.

2. Pat the chicken thighs with paper towels to dry after flattening them. Season with pepper, salt, dried thyme, and garlic powder on the skinless side.

3. Rub butter (1 tablespoon) on each chicken thigh before placing inside the cooking pouch. Vacuum seal
before submerging in the preheated sous vide water
oven. Allow the chicken thighs to cook for one hour
and thirty minutes.

4. Meanwhile, heat a skillet on medium before adding
lard. Once the lard is smoking, add the cooked
chicken thighs. With their skin sides down, cook for
about three to five minutes or until the skins are
crisp. Once done, allow the chicken thighs to drain on
a wire rack after sprinkling the crisped skins with a
little fleur de sel.

5. Place the chicken thighs alongside your favorite vegetables.

6. Serve and enjoy.

Extra Special Turkey

Ingredients:

- Water, filtered (2 quarts)

- Black peppercorns, whole (1 tablespoon)

- Butter (6 tablespoons)

- Turkey, whole, 10-pound (1 piece)

- Kosher salt (11 tablespoons)

- Poultry seasoning (1 tablespoon)

- Sage sprigs, fresh (3 pieces)

Directions:

1. Remove the breasts (with skin on) and leg quarters from the turkey and place in a large bowl; set aside. Reserve the carcass for making turkey stock later.

2. Meanwhile, fill a large pot with water. Add salt, poultry seasoning, and peppercorns; stir to combine.

3. Add the turkey pieces in the pot filled with herbed brine. Cover and place in the refrigerator to brine overnight.

4. Fill the sous vide water oven before preheating to 146 degrees.

5. Meanwhile, pat dry the turkey pieces with paper towels after rinsing well. Place each turkey piece in an in-

dividual cooking pouch. To each pouch, add 1 sage sprig and 2 tablespoons of butter before vacuum sealing.

6. Place the turkey leg quarters in the refrigerator while you cook the turkey breasts first. Submerge the breast pouches in the sous vide water oven; cook for four to six hours. Once done, transfer the breast pouches into an ice bath for a minimum of one hour (alternatively, you can place them in the refrigerator for no more than two days prior to finishing).

7. Raise the sous vide water oven's temperature to 176 degrees. Add the cooking pouches containing the leg quarters and cook for eight to twelve hours. Once done, transfer into an ice bath or refrigerate for one to two days prior to finishing.

8. Fill the sous vide water oven and then preheat to 146 degrees. Drop the breast pouches as well as leg quarter pouches for a minimum of one hour. Once the turkey pieces are reheated, remove from their pouches and pat dry using paper towels. Brush all sides with herbed butter (melted) and set aside.

9. Heat the broiler on high. Cook the turkey pieces for a few minutes or until the skins are seared and golden brown.

10. Serve and enjoy.

Arborio and Cremini Turkey

Ingredients:

- Olive oil, extra virgin (1 teaspoon)

- Garlic, minced, roasted (2 tablespoons)

- Salt, kosher (1/4 teaspoon)

- Pepper, freshly cracked (1/4 teaspoon)

- Cremini mushrooms, cleaned, sliced (10 pieces)

- Rosemary leaves, fresh, minced (1 tablespoon)

- Arborio rice (1 cup)

- Yellow onion, small, peeled, diced (1 piece)

- Turkey, cooked, diced (8 ounces)

- Turkey broth, reduced sodium (3 cups)

- Romano cheese, grated (1/3 cup)

Directions:

1. Fill the sous vide water oven before preheating to 183 degrees.

2. Heat a large skillet over medium. Then add the olive oil. Once heated through, stir in onions and mushrooms. Cook for four to five minutes or until tender and fragrant.

3. Transfer the sautéed onions and mushrooms into a cooking pouch (gallon size). Add all the other ingredients (save for the cheese) for this recipe before vacuum sealing the pouch.

4. Place the sealed pouch in the preheated sous vide water oven. Allow the mixture in the pouch to cook for forty-five minutes. Once done, transfer the pouch contents to a serving bowl (pre-warmed).

5. Use a fork to fluff the cooked rice before stirring in the cheese.

6. Serve right away.

Onion Chicken

Ingredients:

- Mustard oil (3 tablespoons + 1 teaspoon)

- Yogurt, natural, salted (4 ounces)

- Chicken breasts, boneless (2 pounds)

- Cilantro, fresh (a handful)

- Mint leaves, fresh (a handful)

Marinade:

- Ground coriander, powdered (1 tablespoon)

- Fenugreek, dry (1 teaspoon)

- Cilantro, fresh, chopped, divided (1 handful)

- Ginger garlic paste (2 tablespoons)

- Greek yogurt, low-fat, plain (3 tablespoons)

- Garam masala (2 tablespoons)

- Cayenne pepper, ground (1 teaspoon)

- Lemon juice, freshly squeezed (1 tablespoon)

- Food coloring, bright orange (1/4 teaspoon)

- Salt, kosher (1/4 teaspoon)

Onions:

- Fenugreek, dry (1 teaspoon)

- Red onions, large, peeled, sliced thinly (2 pieces)

- Balsamic vinegar (2 tablespoons)

- Olive oil, extra virgin (1 tablespoon)

- Salt, kosher (1/4 teaspoon)

- Brown sugar (1 tablespoon)

Directions:

1. Pat dry the chicken breasts after rinsing, then set aside.

2. Place the ingredients (set aside ½ of the fresh coriander for using later) for the marinade in a large bowl. Add the chicken breasts, turning to ensure all

sides are evenly coated with the marinade. Cover and place in the refrigerator to marinate for two hours.

3. Meanwhile, fill the sous vide water oven and preheat to 160 degrees.

4. Drain off all traces of marinade before placing the chicken breasts inside a cooking pouch. Vacuum seal and then place in the preheated sous vide water oven. Cook for two to three hours.

5. Meanwhile, heat a frying pan (nonstick) on medium-low. Add the olive oil and then stir in the onions. Add the salt and fenugreek, then sauté for about fifteen to twenty minutes or until onions are tender and caramelized. Stir in the balsamic vinegar as well as brown sugar, making sure the onions are well-coated. Once done, remove from heat and set aside.

6. Take the cooked chicken breasts out of the cooking pouch and drain. Pat dry with paper towels and place on a plate.

7. Heat a skillet (nonstick) on medium-high before adding the mustard oil. Once heated through, add the

chicken pieces and cook on each side for one to two minutes or until golden brown and nicely seared.

8. Transfer the chicken pieces onto a platter, alongside the caramelized onions. Top with fresh mint leaves and the reserved fresh coriander.

9. Serve and enjoy.

Easy Herbed Turkey with Cranberry Sauce

Ingredients:

- Salt, kosher (4 tablespoons)

- Butter, unsalted, divided (3 tablespoons)

- Black pepper, freshly ground (1/4 teaspoon)

- Olive oil, extra virgin (1 tablespoon)

- Water (2 cups)

- Black peppercorns (10 pieces)

- Sage leaves, fresh (4 pieces)

- Garlic cloves, roasted, minced finely (2 pieces)

- Cranberry sauce:

- Sugar, granulated (1 cup)

- Cranberries, fresh (12 ounces)

- Orange zest, freshly grated (1 tablespoon)

Directions:

1. Fill the sous vide water oven before preheating to 183 degrees.

2. Fill a cooking pouch with all the ingredients for the cranberry sauce. Vacuum seal before submerging in the preheated sous vide water oven to cook for one hour. Once the mixture is done, take the pouch out of the sous vide water oven and smash gently with your hands to make the cranberry sauce chunky. Quickly submerge the cranberry sauce pouch into an ice bath. After twenty minutes, place in the refrigerator for two to three days.

3. Fill a large cooking pouch (gallon size) with water and salt. Once the salt is dissolved, add the turkey

breast and peppercorns. Vacuum seal the pouch and place in the refrigerator for four hours to allow the turkey to brine.

4. Meanwhile, fill the sous vide water oven and preheat to 146 degrees.

5. Rinse the brined turkey before patting dry with paper towels. Sprinkle black pepper on all sides of the turkey and place inside a cooking pouch. Add butter (2 tablespoons), sage leaves, and garlic before vacuum sealing and submerging in the sous vide water oven. Allow the turkey to cook for three to four hours. Once done, pour the pouch juices into a small bowl and set aside for making gravy/sauce later. Pat dry the chicken pieces and set aside on a large plate.

6. Heat the broiler on high. Meanwhile, brush all surfaces of the cooked turkey with the remaining butter (melted). Broil the turkey for five minutes or until the skin is nicely browned and crisp. Once done, transfer onto a serving platter (warmed).

7. Serve drenched in cranberry sauce. Enjoy.

6 - Mouthwatering Sous Vide Beef for Dinner Recipes

Pesto and Asparagus Beef

Ingredients:

- Basil leaves, fresh (1 cup)

- Salt, kosher, divided (1 tablespoon)

- Lemon zest, freshly grated (1/2 tablespoon)

- Lemon juice, freshly squeezed (1/2 tablespoon)

- Olive oil, extra virgin (1/4 cup)

- Asparagus spears (20 pieces)

- Beef tenderloin, grass-fed, 6-oz. (4 pieces)

- Black pepper, freshly cracked (1/2 teaspoon)

- Garlic cloves, large, fresh, peeled (5 pieces)

- Parmesan cheese, grated (2 tablespoons)

Directions:

1. Fill the sous vide water oven before preheating to 134

degrees.

2. Meanwhile, sprinkle pepper and salt on the meat before placing inside cooking pouches (2 meat portions per pouch). Vacuum seal and then place in the sous vide water oven; allow the meat to cook for two hours.

3. Fill a pot with water and heat on high until boiling. Drop the basil leaves; after thirty seconds, remove and transfer immediately into an ice bath. Wring dry before chopping roughly and set aside in a blender. Do the same to the garlic.

4. In the blender, add the olive oil, salt (1 teaspoon), and Parmesan cheese. Process until well-combined and smooth before adding the lemon juice.

5. Meanwhile, fill a cooking pouch with the asparagus, making sure the asparagus pieces form a single layer. Add a little salt and 1/3 of the basil mixture. Vacuum seal and then drop into the sous vide water oven. Allow the asparagus to cook along with the meat for fifteen minutes. Once done, remove the steak and asparagus from the cooking pouches, and set aside on a

large plate.

6. Heat a grill pan on high before adding a little oil. Once heated through, add the steaks to sear on each side for about thirty to forty-five seconds. Transfer on a platter alongside the asparagus.

7. Serve topped with the remaining basil mixture (2/3 portion) and serve immediately.

Wagyu Fillets with Green Beans

Ingredients:

- Vegetable oil, high smoke point (1 tablespoon)

- Rosemary sprigs, fresh, divided (2 pieces)

- Beef tenderloin filets, Wagyu, 2-inches thick (2 pieces)

- Green beans, cooked (1 ½ cups)

- Butter, unsalted (2 tablespoons)

- Salt, kosher (1/4 teaspoon)

- Pepper, freshly cracked (1/4 teaspoon)

Directions:

1. Fill the sous vide water oven before preheating to 130 degrees. Meanwhile, fill a small cooking pouch with the cooked green beans.

2. Sprinkle pepper and salt on the fillets before placing them inside a cooking pouch (quart-size). After adding a rosemary sprig, vacuum seal the pouch and place in the sous vide water oven. Cook for two hours and thirty minutes to four hours.

3. Thirty minutes before the fillets' cooking time ends, add the pouch containing the green beans to the sous vide water oven.

4. Once done, take the fillets and green beans out of the sous vide water oven and transfer onto large plates. Use paper towels to pat dry the fillets. Set aside.

5. Heat a skillet on high before adding the vegetable oil. Once heated through, add the cooked fillets and sear for one minute on each side. Flip the fillets before adding in the butter as well as remaining rosemary sprig. Cook the fillets in the butter until basted and

crusted on all sides.

6. Serve the fillets alongside green beans and enjoy.

Western Style Burger

Ingredients:

Burger:

- Gorgonzola picante (1 ounce)

- Ground chuck, Angus (10 ounces)

- Frying oil, high smoke point (2 cups)

- Barbecue sauce (2 ounces)

- Butter (1 tablespoon)

- Pork roast (1/2 pound)

- Salt, kosher (1/4 teaspoon)

- Pepper, freshly cracked (1/4 teaspoon)

- Jalapeno peppers, fresh (2 pieces)

- Bread, focaccia (2 pieces)

Onion rings:

- Paprika, Spanish (1/2 tablespoon)

- Cornstarch (1/2 cup)

- Pale ale (15 ounces)

- Cayenne pepper (1/2 teaspoon)

- Baking soda (2 teaspoons)

- Flour, all purpose, bleached (2 cups)

- Black pepper, freshly ground (1 teaspoon)

- Salt, kosher (2 ½ tablespoons)

- Baking powder (2 tablespoons)

- Yellow onion, large, peeled, sliced into quarter-inch slices (1 piece)

Directions:

1. Fill the sous vide water oven before preheating to 140 degrees.

2. Fill a small cooking pouch (quart size) with the pork.

Pour in the barbecue sauce before vacuum sealing the pouch. Drop in the sous vide water oven and allow the pork t cook for one to two days.

3. Sprinkle pepper and salt on the chuck burger, then mold into 2 patties. Place the patties inside a cooking pouch and freeze, unsealed, for two to three hours or until firm.

4. Meanwhile, decrease the water bath temperature to 130 degrees by adding ice cubes or iced water.

5. Take the patties out of the freezer. After vacuum sealing the pouch, place it in the sous vide water oven. Along with the pork, cook the patties for a minimum of one hour.

6. Heat a large skillet on medium-high before adding the oil (2 inches deep). In the meantime, sprinkle the onion slices with pepper and salt before dusting liberally with a small portion of the flour.

7. Place the rest of the flour in a large bowl. Add all the remaining ingredients to the batter. Stir continuously until well-combined and no lumps remain in the pan-

cake batter.

8. Once the oil temperature in the skillet reaches 350 degrees, add the onion slices (after being dipped into the prepared batter) and cook for about two to four minutes or until golden brown and crisp.

9. Remove the cooked onion slices. Add the fresh jalapeno and quickly toss in the oil. Once done (the skin is blistered), transfer onto a small dish.

10. As soon as the burgers are almost done, heat a broiler on high. Add the burgers and briefly cook until nicely seared and a bit charred on the surface.

11. Slice the focaccia into halves, then spread the cut sides with butter. Add to the broiler and sear, butter side down, alongside the burgers.

12. Place the unbuttered focaccia pieces on a platter. Brush a bit of barbecue sauce on the surface before topping with the patties and additional sauce, as well as pork and crumbled gorgonzola. Finish off each burger by adding an onion ring as well as a fried jalapeno and the buttered focaccia half.

13. Serve and enjoy.

Divine Smoked Beef

Ingredients:

- Beef brisket, trimmed (6 pounds)

- Meat rub (1/2 cup) – see below

Meat rub:

- Brown sugar (1 tablespoon)

- Salt, coarse (2 tablespoons)

- Onion powder (1 teaspoon)

- Paprika (3 tablespoons)

- Black pepper, freshly ground (1 tablespoon)

- Garlic powder (1 teaspoon)

- Cumin, ground (1 teaspoon)

Directions:

1. After filling the sous vide water oven with water, set

to 134 degrees to preheat.

2. Follow manufacturer's directions in setting up your device with hickory chips/ cakes/ pellets. For five minutes, use smoke produced by a smoking gun following food preparation.

3. Meanwhile, combine all ingredients for the meat rub in a medium bowl. Use this mixture to coat the brisket generously on all sides.

4. Place the seasoned brisket inside the cooking pouch. Vacuum seal before dropping the pouch inside the sous vide water oven. Allow the brisket to cook for forty-eight hours.

5. Once the brisket is done, remove the cooking pouch from the sous vide water oven and take out the brisket. Place in a closed container and smoke for thirty seconds. Allow the meat to soak up the smoke for five minutes.

6. Meanwhile, heat a skillet on high. Add the smoked brisket and cook for thirty to forty-five seconds or until the surface is crisp, seared, and caramelized.

7. After slicing, serve immediately and enjoy.

Smashing Ribs with Mashers

Ingredients:

Ribs:

- Salt, kosher (1/4 teaspoon)

- Pepper, freshly cracked (1/4 teaspoon)

- Celery stalk, trimmed, diced (1 piece)

- Tomato paste (2 tablespoons)

- Olive oil, extra virgin (1 tablespoon)

- Garlic cloves, peeled, minced (2 pieces)

- Red wine (4 ounces)

- Short ribs, 3-inches (4 pieces)

- Onion, peeled, diced (1/2 piece)

- Carrot, peeled, diced (1 piece)

- Thyme sprig (1 piece)

- Oil – to be used in searing

Mashers:

- Salt, kosher (1/4 teaspoon)

- Pepper, freshly cracked (1/4 teaspoon)

- Cream (2 ounces)

- Cheddar cheese (2 ounces)

- Red potatoes, creamer (1 pound)

- Butter (2 ounces)

- Chives, fresh, minced (1 tablespoon)

Directions:

1. Fill the sous vide water oven with water before setting to 185 degrees to preheat.

2. Rub pepper and salt on the short ribs, making sure all sides are seasoned well.

3. Heat a skillet (nonstick) on medium-high before adding the oil. Once heated through, add the

seasoned short ribs and cook until all sides are seared and browned. Once the ribs are done, transfer to a plate and cover to keep warm.

4. Wipe the pan before adding in olive oil (1 table-spoon). Stir in the vegetables and sauté until browned. Stir in the tomato paste as well and cook for one minute before pouring in the wine. Lower heat to medium and allow mixture to simmer until reduced. Transfer the mixture to a large bowl and place in the refrigerator for thirty minutes.

5. Pour the vegetable mixture into a cooking pouch. Add the ribs on top, making sure they form a single layer. Vacuum seal the pouch and place inside the sous vide water oven to cook for twelve hours.

6. Meanwhile, place the potatoes at the bottom of a cooking pouch. Sprinkle in the seasoning before vacuum sealing and dropping into the sous vide water oven. Allow the potatoes to cook for one hour before taking out of the water oven. Roughly press on the cooked potatoes (through the pouch) until mashed before slipping in the remaining ingredients. Mix well

and divide the potato mixture among 4 individual plates.

7. Take the cooked ribs out of the sous vide water oven. Place one rib on top of each masher-filled plate.

8. Meanwhile, pour the rib juices (from the pouch in which you cooked the ribs) into a pan. Heat on medium and cook until reduced. Drizzle the reduced liquid on top of the ribs.

9. Serve and enjoy.

7 - Scrumptious Sous Vide Pork for Dinner Recipes

Barbecue Pork Ribs

Ingredients:

- Olive oil, extra virgin – for cooking

- Ribs, country style, meaty (8 pieces)

- Barbecue sauce – see below

- Barbecue sauce:

- Salad oil (1 cup)

- Garlic, granulated (3 tablespoons)

- Pepper, white (2 tablespoons)

- Lemon juice (4 tablespoons)

- Salt, kosher (3 tablespoons)

- Ketchup (114 ounces)

- Cumin, ground (2 tablespoons)

- Oregano, dry (2 teaspoons)

7 - SCRUMPTIOUS SOUS VIDE PORK FOR DINNER RE-CIPES

- Molasses (1 cup)

- Black pepper, freshly ground (1 tablespoon)

- Onions, medium, peeled, minced (4 pieces)

- Brown sugar (2 ½ pounds)

- Cider vinegar (1 quart)

- Mustard, dry (4 tablespoons)

- Chile powder (1/3 cup)

- Cayenne pepper (1 tablespoon)

- Tabasco sauce (3 ounces)

- Honey (1 cup)

- Thyme, dry (1 tablespoon)

Meat rub:

- Sugar, granulated (2 tablespoons)

- Chile powder (2 tablespoons)

- Cayenne pepper (2 teaspoons)

- Cumin (2 tablespoons)

- Black pepper, freshly ground (1 tablespoon)

- Salt, kosher (1/4 cup)

- Paprika (2 tablespoons)

- Garlic powder (2 tablespoons)

- Mustard powder (1 tablespoon)

Directions:

1. Heat a soup pot (large) on medium before adding the salad oil. Once heated through, stir in the onions as well as brown sugar (1 tablespoon). Cook for five minutes or until the onions are caramelized.

2. Add the rest of the barbecue ingredients. Then stir well until the mixture is evenly combined. Turn heat down to low and allow the mixture to simmer for about an hour. Once done, pour the barbecue sauce into an airtight jar and place in the refrigerator.

3. Meanwhile, fill the sous vide water oven before pre-heating to 160 degrees.

4. Fill a small mixing bowl with the ingredients for the rib rub, Stir to combine and set aside.

5. Drizzle olive oil on the ribs before liberally brushing all sides with the prepared rib rub. Place the ribs inside large cooking pouches, making sure they form a single layer and then vacuum seal.

6. Drop the cooking pouches into the sous vide water oven. Allow the ribs to cook for eighteen to twenty-four hours.

7. Once the ribs are done, remove from the cooking pouches and set on a platter. Smother with the barbecue sauce and serve immediately.

Veggies and Pork with Blueberry Sauce and Sweet Potato Puree

Ingredients:

- Pork belly slab, 8-oz. (1 piece)

- Marinade:

- Cumin (1 teaspoon)

- Black pepper, freshly cracked (1 teaspoon)

- Fennel seeds (1 teaspoon)

- Cayenne pepper (1 tablespoon)

- Olive oil, extra virgin (1/4 cup)

- Salt, kosher (2 teaspoons)

- Cinnamon (1 tablespoon)

- Cloves, whole (3 pieces)

- Soy sauce, reduced sodium (1/2 cup)

Sweet potato puree:

- Butter, unsalted (2 tablespoons)

- Sweet potato, white, peeled, diced (1 piece)

- Cream (1/4 cup)

- Blueberry sauce:

- Sugar (1/4 cup)

- Vegetable stock (1/4 cup)

- Butter, unsalted (1 tablespoon)

- Blueberries, fresh/ frozen (1/2 cup)

- Soy sauce, low sodium (1 splash)

- Sesame chili oil (1/2 teaspoon)

Veggies:

- Mushrooms, wood ear (8 pieces)

- Mushrooms, nameko (4 ounces)

- Peppers, shishito (8 pieces)

- Vegetable stock (1 tablespoon)

- Butter, unsalted (1 tablespoon)

Directions:

1. Place the pork belly in a large bowl. Season with a mixture of pepper, cayenne, salt, cumin, and cinnamon. Add the fennel seeds, cloves, olive oil, and soy sauce, then toss until well-combined. Cover and place in the refrigerator to marinate overnight.

2. Fill the sous vide water oven before preheating to 155
   degrees.

3. Remove the marinated pork belly from the refrigerator. Drain the marinade and then pat the meat with
   paper towels to dry. Transfer into a cooking pouch,
   vacuum seal, and drop into the sous vide water oven.
   Allow the pork belly to cook for four hours.

4. Meanwhile, heat a large pot on medium-high. Add
   salt (1 teaspoon) and bring water to a boil. Once boiling, add the potatoes; return to boiling and cook until
   tender.

5. Once the potatoes are done, strain and place in the
   food processor. Add salt, cream, and butter, then process until the potato mixture is well-combined. Return to the pot (after discarding the water) and heat
   on low to keep warm until served.

6. Heat a saucepot (1-quart) on medium-high before
   adding the sugar and blueberries. Once the sugar be-
   gins melting, gently mash the blueberries. Stir in the
   vegetable stock as well as sesame chili oil and soy
   sauce; cook for about two minutes or until heated

through.

7. Transfer the blueberry mixture into the food processor. Process until well-blended and then strain into the saucepot. Heat on medium and allow the blueberry mixture to cook until reduced to 1/2 and thickened. Once done, remove from heat and set aside.

8. Heat a saucepan on high before adding a little oil. Once heated through, stir in the shishito peppers as well as mushrooms. Cook for one minute before stirring in the vegetable stock (1 tablespoon). Allow the entire mixture to cook until reduced. Then stir in the butter (1 tablespoon). Once the butter has melted into the mixture, remove from heat and set aside.

9. Once the pork belly is done, remove from the sous vide water oven and cooking pouch, then transfer onto a plate. Set the pouch juices aside in a covered container.

10. Meanwhile, heat a frying pan on high before adding oil. Once the oil is heated through, add the pork belly and cook until the skin is seared. Gradually add the

reserved pouch juices and continue cooking until the pork belly is basted and its skin is crispy.

11. Serve and enjoy.

Brazilian Style Black Bean Stew

Ingredients:

- Onion, small, peeled, chopped (1 piece)

- Tomatoes, medium, trimmed, diced (3 pieces)

- Pork ribs, meaty, cooked, w/ meat pulled from bone (4 pieces)

- Sweet potato, medium, peeled, sliced (1 piece)

- Black beans, rinsed well (1 cup)

- Mango, peeled, seeded, cubed (1 piece)

- Bacon slices, thick, diced (4 pieces)

- Garlic clove, peeled, minced (1 piece)

- Red bell pepper, small, stemmed, seeded, diced (1 piece)

- Stock, vegetable/ stock (3 cups)

- Salt, kosher (1/4 teaspoon)

- Pepper, freshly cracked (1/4 teaspoon)

- Sausages, sweet, cooked, sliced (2 pieces)

Garnish:

- Arroz Braziliero, cooked (2 cups)

- Cilantro, fresh, chopped (a handful)

- Orange, fresh, sliced (1 piece)

Directions:

1. Fill the sous vide water oven before preheating to 195
   degrees.

2. Meanwhile, heat a skillet on medium. Once hot, add
   the bacon and cook until browned and crisp.

3. Stir in the garlic and onions; cook for an additional
   two minutes or until fragrant and translucent. Turn
   off heat and allow the bacon mixture to slightly cool
   down.

4. Fill a large cooking pouch (1 gallon) with the bacon mixture as well as tomatoes, sweet potatoes, black beans, salt, pepper, red bell pepper, and vegetable stock. Vacuum seal before submerging into the pre-heated sous vide water oven and cook for three hours.

5. Meanwhile, fill another cooking pouch with the mangoes and cooked meats. Vacuum seal and drop into the sous vide water oven (after lowering its temperature to 158 degrees). Allow to warm along with the beans for half an hour.

6. Once done, transfer everything into a tureen (warmed). Stir to combine all cooked items. Serve topped with cilantro, orange, and Arroz Braziliero.

7. Enjoy.

Sage and Rosemary Pork Belly with Onions and Potatoes

Ingredients:

- Pork belly, rind on (1 pound)

- Olive oil, extra virgin (1 tablespoon)

- Sage, fresh, chopped roughly (1 teaspoon)

- Sea salt (1/4 teaspoon)

- Black pepper, freshly ground (1/4 teaspoon)

- Rosemary leaves, fresh (1 teaspoon)

Potatoes:

- White onion, medium, peeled, minced (1 piece)

- White wine, dry (1/2 cup)

- Sea salt (1/4 teaspoon)

- Pepper, freshly cracked (1/4 teaspoon)

- Olive oil, extra virgin (3 tablespoons)

- Potatoes, medium, peeled, chopped (3 pieces)

- Broth, beef, reduced sodium (2 cups)

Onions:

- Olive oil, extra virgin (4 tablespoons + 1 tablespoon)

- Water, filtered (2 ½ cups)

- Sea salt (1/4 teaspoon)

- Pepper, freshly cracked (1/4 teaspoon)

- Onions, cipollini, peeled (12 pieces)

- Vinegar, white wine (1/2 cup)

- Vinegar, balsamic (1 tablespoon)

Directions:

1. Heat a skillet on medium before adding the oil. Sauté for about five minutes or until a bit golden. Season with pepper and salt before pouring in the vinegar. Add the sugar as well. Then stir everything to combine. Allow the mixture to cook for five minutes or until all traces of vinegar are gone. Add water before covering and reducing heat to low. After five minutes, transfer the onions into a skillet greased with a little olive oil and heated on high. Add balsamic vinegar then cook until caramelized. Pour into a medium bowl and set aside.

2. Heat a medium gauge pot (heavy bottomed) on low before adding oil. Stir in the onion and cook for six to

eight minutes or until softened and fragrant. Stir in the potatoes and cook for another five minutes, making sure they are evenly coated. Pour in the white wine, stir, and allow to evaporate before pouring in the broth. Cook until the entire mixture is heated through and the potatoes are tender. Season with pepper and salt, then process into a puree with an immersion blender, food processor, or blender. Set aside in a large bowl.

3. Fill the sous vide water oven before preheating to 147 degrees.

4. Meanwhile, place the ingredients for the seasoning in a medium bowl. Stir to combine. Then rub the mixture all over the pork belly. Place the pork belly inside a cooking pouch, then vacuum seal and place in the preheated sous vide water oven to cook for eighteen to twenty-four hours.

5. Once the pork belly is done, take it out of the pouch and slice into 4 one-inch-thick portions. Set aside on a plate.

6. In the meantime, heat a heavy skillet (cast iron) on

high. Add olive oil and once heated through, add the pork belly with its rind side down. Cook until the rind is nicely seared, crunchy and golden.

7. Serve and enjoy.

Grilled Pork Ribs

Ingredients:

- Pork ribs, boneless (1 pound)

- Oregano, Mexican (1 tablespoon)

- Garlic cloves, peeled, chopped (2 pieces)

- Orange juice, freshly squeezed (1 cup)

- Onion, purple, peeled, sliced into rounds (1/2 piece)

- Achiote paste (2 ounces)

- Sazon seasoning, w/ salt, pepper & cumin (1 tablespoon)

- Vinegar, apple cider (1/2 cup)

- Olive oil, extra virgin (1/2 cup)

- Orange, sliced into rounds (1 piece)

Directions:

1. Fill the sous vide water oven before preheating to 149 degrees.

2. Pour the orange juice into a large bowl. Add the achiote paste, Sazon seasoning, and oregano, then whisk to combine into a smooth paste. Pour in the vinegar and whisk again to combine. Set aside.

3. Fill a large cooking pouch with the ribs. Pour in the prepared marinade as well as olive oil and garlic. Vacuum seal before submerging the pouch into the sous vide water oven. Allow the ribs to cook for twenty-four to forty-eight hours.

4. Heat a grill pan on high after generously oiling it. Once the ribs are tenderly done, transfer from the pouch and onto the grill pan to cook until both sides are seared.

5. Serve pork ribs with veggies on the side. Enjoy.

8 - Appetizing Sous Vide Lamb for Dinner Recipes

Lamb with Heirloom Tomatoes

Ingredients:

- Cherry tomatoes (1 pint)

- Salt, kosher, divided (1 tablespoon)

- Olive oil, extra virgin (1/4 cup)

- Rosemary sprigs, fresh (2 pieces)

- Chile flakes (1 teaspoon)

- Lamb rack, fresh (1 piece)

- Black pepper, freshly ground (1 teaspoon)

- Mint (1/2 bunch)

- Garlic cloves, peeled (2 pieces)

Directions:

1. Fill the sous vide water oven and then preheat to 136 degrees.

2. Meanwhile, sprinkle pepper and salt on the lamb, making sure all sides are evenly coated. Place inside a cooking pouch along with the rosemary sprigs, before vacuum sealing.

3. Drop the cooking pouch into the sous vide water oven. Allow the lamb to cook for two hours.

4. In the meantime, heat a pan on medium before adding olive oil. Add the garlic (thinly sliced), stir, and simmer for about three minutes. Once done, transfer into a cooking pouch along with the tomatoes, remaining salt, chile flakes, and mint. Vacuum seal and drop into the sous vide water oven as well to cook for one hour.

5. Once the lamb and tomato mixture are both done, remove from their pouches and transfer onto plates.

6. Heat a generously oiled grill pan on high before adding the lamb. Cook until all sides are seared, then transfer onto a platter. Set aside.

7. Meanwhile, drain the oil from the cooked tomatoes. After discarding the mint, place the tomatoes along-

side the lamb.

8. Serve and enjoy.

Lamb with Fig Syrup

Ingredients:

Lamb:

- Garlic cloves, peeled, minced (2 pieces)

- Cayenne, divided (1 teaspoon)

- Fennel pollen (2 tablespoons)

- Lamb racks, half ribs (2 pieces)

- Vegetable oil (1/4 cup)

- Rosemary, chopped finely (4 tablespoons)

- Black pepper, freshly ground (1 teaspoon)

- Salt, kosher, divided (2 ½ teaspoons)

Syrup:

- Fig preserves (1/2 cup)

8 - APPETIZING SOUS VIDE LAMB FOR DINNER RE-CIPES

- Vinegar, champagne (1/4 cup)

- Maple syrup, pure (1/4 cup)

Garnish:

- Walnuts, roasted, chopped finely (4 ounces)

- Goat cheese, young, crumbled (10 ounces)

- Parsley, Italian, chopped roughly (5 tablespoons)

Directions:

1. Fill the sous vide water oven before preheating to 134 degrees.

2. Place salt (2 teaspoons), garlic, pepper, cayenne (1/2 teaspoon), oil, fennel pollen, and rosemary in a medium bowl. Stir to combine.

3. Pat the lamb racks with paper towels to dry before rubbing the prepared spice mixture on all sides. Place inside a cooking pouch, then vacuum seal and submerge in the preheated sous vide water oven. Allow the lamb racks to cook for eighteen hours.

4. Meanwhile, fill a large saucepan (heavy bottomed)

with vinegar, salt (1/2 teaspoon), maple syrup, cayenne (1/2 teaspoon), and fig preserves. Stir to combine and then heat on medium. Allow the mixture to simmer before removing from heat and setting aside.

5. Once the lamb racks are done, remove from the sous vide water oven. Open the cooking pouch and slip the racks onto a large plate.

6. Heat a grill on high after generously greasing it with oil. Coat the lamb racks with fig syrup before cooking on the grill until nicely seared and browned.

7. Transfer the grilled lamb racks onto a platter. Coat again with fig syrup before slicing between the bones.

8. Transfer the ribs onto individual plates, making sure the ribs are evenly stacked. Top with chopped walnuts, crumbled goat cheese, and Italian parsley.

9. Serve and enjoy.

Pomegranate-Coffee Lamb

Ingredients:

- Brown sugar, packed (1/4 cup)

- Pepper, freshly cracked (1/4 teaspoon)

- Salt, kosher (1/4 teaspoon)

- Pomegranate juice (2 cups)

- Butter (1 tablespoon)

- Coffee, warm (1 cup)

- Balsamic vinegar (1/4 cup)

- Lamb racks, 1-oz. (2 pieces)

- Rosemary sprigs, fresh (2 pieces)

Directions:

- Place the brown sugar in a large bowl. Add the warm coffee and stir well. Once all the sugar granules are completely dissolved, add the pomegranate juice and balsamic vinegar. Stir again until well-combined, then reserve one cup of the mixture for using later (place in a small covered bowl and refrigerate).

- Place the 2 lamb racks in a large cooking pouch. Pour

in the remaining marinade and vacuum seal. Place in the refrigerator to marinate for four to twelve hours.

- Meanwhile, fill the sous vide water oven before pre-heating to 132 degrees.

- Drain the marinated lamb racks. Then pat dry with paper towels to remove any excess marinade. Season all sides of the racks with pepper and salt before placing into separate cooking pouches (gallon size). Include a fresh rosemary sprig in each cooking pouch before vacuum sealing, then drop into the sous vide water oven. Let the lamb racks cook for two hours.

- Meanwhile, take the reserved marinate out of the refrigerator. Pour into a skillet and heat on medium. Allow the marinade to boil before cooking for another five minutes or until reduced and thickened. Add the salt (1/8 teaspoon) and butter, whisk well until well-combined, and set aside.

- Set the broiler on high to preheat.

- Take the lamb pouches out if the sous vide water oven. Remove the racks from their pouches and transfer to a large pan (broiler safe). Cook under the broiler for four to five minutes or until all sides are seared and browned.

- Place the broiled lamb racks in the skillet where you cooked the sauce. Turn the racks to make sure all sides are evenly coated. Then slice each rack into single chops.

- Serve right away with additional sauce on the side.

- Enjoy.

Salsa Verde Lamb Croquettes

Ingredients:

- Olive oil, extra virgin – as needed in cooking

- Thyme sprigs, fresh (4 pieces)

- Eggs, beaten slightly w/ 1 tbsp. of water (2 pieces)

- Pepper, freshly cracked (1/4 teaspoon)

- Breadcrumbs, panko (1 cup)

- Veal demi-glace (1/4 cup)

- Flour, all-purpose (1/4 cup) – for dusting before breading

- Lamb shanks (2 pieces)

- Salt, kosher (1/4 teaspoon)

- Salsa verde – see below

Salsa verde:

- Parsley, fresh, chopped coarsely (1 cup)

- Lemon zest, freshly grated (1 tablespoon)

- Salt, kosher (1/4 teaspoon)

- Basil, fresh, chopped (2 tablespoons)

- Olive oil, extra virgin (2/3 cup)

- Garlic cloves, medium, unpeeled (6 pieces)

- Anchovy fillets, blotted w/ paper towels to remove oil (4 pieces)

- Tarragon, fresh, chopped (1 tablespoon)

- Egg yolks (3 pieces)

- Pepper, freshly ground (1/4 teaspoon)

Directions:

1. Fill a small saucepan with cold water (1/2 inch deep). Add the garlic and cover the pan before heating on high. Once boiling, discard the water and add fresh water (1/2 inch deep). Allow to boil again before removing the garlic and rinsing under cold water. Once the garlic is cool enough to work with, remove its skin and chop into bits.

2. Place the chopped garlic in the food processor. Add the lemon zest, anchovies, tarragon, parsley, egg yolks, and basil. Process while you gradually stream in the oil. Once the mixture is just blended (it should not be smooth), add pepper and salt to season. Set aside.

3. Meanwhile, fill the sous vide water oven and preheat to 144 degrees.

4. Rub oil on the shanks before seasoning with pepper and salt. Place the seasoned shanks inside a cooking pouch (large). Add 2 sprigs of thyme into each pouch

before vacuum sealing. Place in the preheated sous vide water oven and allow to cook for forty-eight hours. Once done, drain the pouch juices into a covered bowl and set aside in the refrigerator. Transfer the shanks onto a platter, separate the meat from the bones, cover, and set aside.

5. Pour the reserved pouch juices in a saucepan and heat on medium. Stir and cook until reduced and thickened, then pour into a sauce pot. Stir in the glace and simmer on low. Once the sauce is thick enough that it sticks to a spoon, add in the lamb meat. Stir to combine, making sure the meat is evenly coated with the sauce.

6. Divide the meat into four equal portions. Place each lamb meat portion on a sheet of cling film. Then roll to form a tight cylindrical shape. Place all rolled lamb meats in the refrigerator to chill overnight.

7. Take the chilled lamb cylinders out of their wraps and set on a plate. Meanwhile, fill 3 separate bowls with panko crumbs, egg wash, and flour. Coat the lamb cylinders with the flour before dipping into egg wash.

Transfer into the bowl containing the panko crumbs and dredge, then place on a large plate.

8. Heat a deep fryer on high before adding the oil. Once the oil reaches 165 degrees, add the breaded lamb cylinders and cook until golden brown. Place on layers of paper towels to drain.

9. Serve lamb croquettes with the prepared salsa verde.

10. Enjoy.

Lamb with Cabbage and Potato Fondants

Ingredients:

Lamb:

- Salt, kosher (1/4 teaspoon)

- Pepper, freshly cracked (1/4 teaspoon)

- Lamb rump steaks, 8-oz. (4 pieces)

- Red currant jelly (2 tablespoons)

Cabbage:

- Leeks (2 pieces)

- Olive oil, extra virgin (3 tablespoons)

- Double cream (10 ounces)

- Mustard, whole grain (1 teaspoon)

- Cabbage head, Savoy (1 piece)

- Pancetta, smoked (7 ounces)

- Chicken stock, reduced sodium (8 ounces)

- Butter (2 tablespoons)

Potato fondants:

- Butter (10 tablespoons)

- Garlic cloves, peeled (3 pieces)

- Potatoes, Maris Piper (8 pieces)

- Chicken stock (14 ounces)

- Thyme sprig, fresh (1 piece)

Directions:

8 - APPETIZING SOUS VIDE LAMB FOR DINNER RE-CIPES

1. Fill the sous vide water oven before preheating to 135 degrees. Set the conventional oven to 395 degrees to preheat as well.

2. Peel the potatoes before slicing into equal-sized barrel/ cylindrical shapes. Place in a medium bowl.

3. Meanwhile, heat a roasting tray on high. Add the butter and allow to melt and foam before adding the potatoes. Cook for two to three minutes or until all sides are cooked through and golden brown.

4. Stir in the garlic as well as thyme. Pour in the chicken stock and mix well before transferring the roasting tray into the preheated conventional oven. Cook for about forty-five minutes or until the potatoes are tender, moist, and cooked through.

5. Sprinkle pepper and steaks on the rump steaks before placing inside cooking pouches. Vacuum seal and place in the preheated sous vide water oven and allow to cook for forty-five minutes to one hour.

6. Discard the cabbage's outer leaves and hard stalk before slicing into fine shreds. Set aside in a small bowl.

7. Meanwhile, heat a frying pan on medium. Add oil and allow to get extremely hot before adding the pancetta. Cook until nicely crisp and golden. Stir in the butter; once foaming, stir in the cabbage and leeks as well. Sprinkle pepper and salt and fry for about three to four more minutes or until the cabbage and leeks are softened and a bit golden.

8. Pour in the stock. Allow the mixture to cook for an additional five minutes or until the leeks and cabbage and cooked through and tender. Add the mustard and double cream, then cook for another five minutes or until the mixture is reduced to ¾ its original volume. Cover to keep warm.

9. Once the rump steaks are done, remove from the sous vide water oven and transfer onto a plate. Pat dry with paper towels and set aside.

10. In the meantime, heat a pan on high. Once extremely hot, add the rump steaks and cook until both sides are browned. Place on a platter and set aside.

11. Turn the heat of the same pan down to low before adding in the currant jelly. Allow to melt and then

brush on the rump steaks, making sure all sides are evenly coated. Cut the glazed rump steaks to form 8 slices.

12. Divide the cabbage among 4 plates. Top each with 2 rump steak slices and serve alongside the potato fondants.

13. Enjoy.

9 - Delicious Sous Vide Duck for Dinner Recipes

Duck Breast with Farro and Blackberry Jam

Ingredients:

Duck breast:

- Thyme leaves, fresh, picked (1/2 tablespoon)

- Black pepper, freshly ground (1/4 teaspoon)

- Red onions, julienned (1 cup)

- Salt, kosher (1/4 teaspoon)

- Garlic clove, peeled, smashed (1 piece)

- Parsley, chopped (1 tablespoon)

- Duck breasts, 8-oz. (2 pieces)

- Thyme sprigs, fresh, divided (4 pieces)

- Olive oil, extra virgin (1 tablespoon)

- Brown sugar (1 tablespoon)

- Baby escarole heads, cut, washed (3 pieces)

- Shallots, minced (1 teaspoon)

- Farro, cooked (1 cup) – see below

Farro:

- Olive oil, extra virgin (1 tablespoon)

- Stock, chicken/ duck (2 cups)

- Carrot, peeled, diced finely (1/2 piece)

- Salt, kosher (1 teaspoon)

- Farro (3/4 cup)

- Celery stalk, trimmed, diced finely (1/2 piece)

- Turnip, peeled, diced finely (1/4 piece)

Blackberry jam:

- Sugar, granulated (3/4 cup)

- Blackberries, fresh (1 ¼ pounds)

- Lemon juice, freshly squeezed (1/2 tablespoon)

Directions:

1. Place the berries in a colander and rinse under cool water. Transfer into a large bowl and toss gently with sugar. Over the bowl and place in the refrigerator; allow the berries to marinate overnight. Heat a large saucepan over medium. Then add the marinated berries to warm and soften. Remove the seeds with a food mill/ fine-mesh sieve before returning to the pan. Heat on medium, cook until thickened and keep warm.

2. Heat a saucepan on medium-high. Add the farro and cook until lightly toasted. Stir in the oil, carrot, celery, and turnip; cook for two minutes or until a bit tender. Pour in the water and add in salt. Stir to combine and allow the mixture to boil before reducing heat to medium-low. Cover and simmer for half an hour or until a small amount of liquid remains. Once done, fluff the farro with a fork and set aside.

3. Heat a saucepan on medium-high before adding the oil (1 tablespoon). Once heated through, stir in the onions. Arrange the onions into an even layer before

sprinkling the brown sugar on top. Stir and cook until the onions are tender and browned, then place in a covered bowl and refrigerate.

4. Fill the sous vide water oven and preheat to 132 degrees.

5. Sprinkle black pepper on the duck breasts before placing inside a cooking pouch. Add a thyme sprig on top of each duck breast. Vacuum seal the cooking pouch before submerging in the sous vide water oven. Allow the duck breasts to cook for thirty minutes to two hours. Once done, remove from the cooking pouch and transfer onto a plate; pat dry with paper towels, season with salt, and set aside. Meanwhile, pour the pouch juices into a small bowl and reserve.

6. Heat a large sauté pan on medium before adding the olive oil. Once heated through, stir in the garlic clove as well as the rest of the thyme sprigs. Once the oil starts smoking, turn heat down to low and add the duck breasts. Cook with their skin sides down for seven minutes. Once the fat is rendered, pour it off the pan. Flip the duck breasts on the other side to

cook for an additional minute. Once done, place on a platter, cover, and let sit.

7. Discard the fat from the pan and return to the stove. Heat on medium-high before adding the escarole. Cook until caramelized and a bit wilted. Then pour in the reserved pouch juices. Add the farro and caramelized onions as well as the shallots and garlic; stir and cook until the entire mixture is warmed through. Stir in thyme and parsley before covering to keep warm.

8. Drizzle the prepared blackberry sauce on the plate to form streaks. Place a small mound of farro and escarole mixture on one side, and top with the sliced duck breast. Add fresh thyme leaves and serve immediately.

Peking Style Duck Legs and Eggs

Ingredients:

Duck legs:

- Duck fat (8 tablespoons)

- Duck legs (8 pieces)

- Oil, high smoke point – for deep frying

Duck eggs:

- Duck eggs (6 pieces)

Cucumber spaghetti:

- Soya sauce, dark (2 teaspoons)

- Ginger, fresh, grated finely (1 teaspoon)

- Sesame oil (1 tablespoon)

- Cucumber (1 piece)

- Balsamic vinegar (2 teaspoons)

- Garlic clove, peeled, grated finely (1 piece)

Spring onion puree:

- Onions, Spanish, peeled, sliced finely (3 pieces)

- Spring onions, green, washed, sliced thinly (6 bunches)

- Pomace oil (2 tablespoons)

- Double cream (10 ounces)

- Salt, kosher (1/4 teaspoon)

Dressing:

- Honey (1/4 cup)

- Soya sauce, dark (1/4 cup)

- Sesame oil (1 tablespoon)

- Ketchup (8 ounces)

- Orange juice, freshly squeezed (1/4 cup)

- Oyster sauce (1/4 cup)

Pancake crumb:

- Salt, kosher (1/4 teaspoon)

- Pastry sheets, feuille de brick, torn into bits (3 pieces)

Directions:

1. Fill the sous vide water oven before preheating to 180 degrees.

2. Fill 2 cooking pouches (large) with the duck legs (4 legs into 1 pouch). Pour in the duck fat before vacuum sealing the pouches, then place in the sous vide water oven. Allow the duck legs to cook for twelve hours.

3. Once the dusk legs are done, remove from the pouches and place on top of paper towels to drain off excess fat. Separate the meat (while still warm) from the bone and shred into thin strips before placing in a covered bowl. Set aside.

4. Turn the sous vide water oven temperature down to 147 degrees. Gently submerge the duck eggs to cook for one hour and ten minutes.

5. Meanwhile, heat a saucepan on medium before adding pomace oil; spread to form a thin film on the pan surface. Stir in the Spanish onions as well as salt (a pinch). Allow the onions to sweat for about four to five minutes or until translucent and softened.

6. Stir in the cream before turning the heat up to medium-high and allowing the mixture to boil. Stir in the spring onions; cook for about two to three minutes or until tender. Pour the mixture into the

blender and process until well-combined and smooth. Transfer the puree to a large bowl and place in the refrigerator.

7. After peeling and deseeding the cucumber, cut into long, extremely thin strands. Place in a large bowl and set aside.

8. Place all the ingredients for the cucumber strands in a small bowl. Stir to combine and set aside (toss with the cucumber later). Do the same with the ingredients for preparing the duck dressing.

9. Heat a deep fryer before adding the oil. Once the oil is heated to 356 degrees, add the shredded duck leg and cook until crispy. Once done, transfer onto a plate lined with paper towels and set aside.

10. Add pastry pieces to the same heated oil. Cook for half a minute, drain, and season with a bit of salt. Set aside.

11. Heat the pureed spring onion until warmed through, then divide among 4 plates. Gently toss the crispy duck meat with ½ of the dressing; divide among 4

portions and place each onto one plate (on top of the pureed spring onion).

12. Finish each plate by adding one duck egg, ¼ of the dressed cucumber strands, ¼ of the pancake crumbs, and ¼ of the remaining duck dressing.

13. Serve and enjoy.

Juniper Berry Duck

Ingredients:

- Thyme sprigs, fresh (3 pieces)

- Juniper berries, fresh-dried, red raisin (1/2 cup)

- Duck leg, quarter (1 piece)

- Salt, kosher (1/4 teaspoon)

- Spinach, fresh (1 cup)

- Orange zest, freshly grated (1 tablespoon)

- Orange fruit (1 piece)

Directions:

1. Fill the sous vide water oven before preheating to 165 degrees.

2. Place the duck leg in a large bowl. Rub salt all over its sides before setting aside.

3. Use a vegetable peeler to strip off the zest from the orange. Section the fruit and place in a small bowl.

4. Place the juniper berries on a sheet of cling film. Top with the orange zest as well as thyme sprigs before loosely rolling. Place inside a small cooking pouch (quart size) and then top with a layer of orange sections. Add the salted duck leg in the middle before vacuum sealing the pouch.

5. Squeeze the orange pieces through the pouch before dropping the pouch into the sous vide water oven. Cook the duck leg for five to eight hours.

6. Once the duck leg is done, remove from the sous vide water oven. Drain the pouch juices into a skillet; set aside.

7. Meanwhile, set the broiler on high to preheat.

8. Unroll the juniper berry wrap and transfer the contents into the skillet containing the pouch juices. Heat on medium and cook the mixture until reduced. Season with pepper and salt, remove from heat and set aside.

9. Place the cooked duck leg below the preheated broiler to sear. Once done, transfer onto a platter.

10. Serve the broiled duck leg alongside a mound of fresh spinach. Smother with orange sauce and enjoy.

Easy Seared Duck

Ingredients:

- Shallots, chopped (2 tablespoons)

- Broccoli stalks, Chinese (2 pieces)

- Duck breasts, 8-oz. (4 pieces)

- Red wine (2 tablespoons)

Marinade:

- Cinnamon sticks (2 pieces)

- Tong kwai herb (4 pieces)

- Sugar (1 teaspoon)

- Spring onions, green (2 pieces)

- Star anise pods (2 pieces)

- Ginger, fresh, minced (2 coins)

- Garlic cloves, peeled, mashed (4 pieces)

- Salt, kosher (1 teaspoon)

Ginger water:

- Water, filtered (3 ¼ ounces)

- Sugar (1/2 teaspoon)

- Ginger, sliced (3 ¼ ounces)

- Rice wine, Chinese (3 ¼ ounces)

- Salt, kosher (1/2 teaspoon)

Reduction base:

- Chicken, roasted (1/2 piece)

- Oyster sauce (2 teaspoons)

- Onion, large, peeled, sliced, sautéed (1/4 piece)

- Soy sauce, light (5 ounces)

- Chicken stock, reduced sodium (5 ounces)

- Apple, large, peeled, sliced, sautéed (1/4 piece)

Directions:

1. Place the duck breast inside a cooking pouch. Add the ingredients for the marinade before vacuum sealing and placing in the refrigerator to marinate overnight.

2. Fill the sous vide water oven and preheat to 133 degrees.

3. Add the duck breast pouch into the sous vide water oven and cook for fifty minutes.

4. Pour water into the blender. Add the ginger and process until well-combined into a paste. Pass the ginger paste through a sieve and set aside the liquid in a small bowl.

5. Fill a saucepan with the Chinese wine. Add the re-

served ginger liquid and stir to combine. Stir in the salt and sugar before heating the saucepan on medium-high. Allow the mixture to boil and then set aside.

6. Pour the ingredients for the reduction base into a pot. Stir to combine, heat on medium-high, and allow the mixture to simmer for an hour or until reduced to 2/3 its original volume. Pour into a sieve set atop a medium bowl; set aside.

7. Fill a pot with water and heat on medium-high. Once boiling, add the gai lan yo blanch for one minute. Remove and set aside in a small bowl.

8. Heat a skillet on medium-high before adding the shallots. Once fragrant, pour in the red wine as well as reduction base (100 milliliters). Stir and cook until the mixture is reduced to 2/3 its original amount. Remove from heat and set aside.

9. Meanwhile, heat a skillet on medium. Add the duck breast and cook until seared and browned on both sides. Once done, transfer to a plate.

10. Serve the duck leg alongside the blanched gai lan and topped with the reduction sauce.

Ginger Garlic Duck Breasts

Ingredients:

- Ginger garlic paste (4 teaspoons)

- Shallots, peeled (6 ounces)

- Coriander powder, ground (2 teaspoons)

- Coconut milk (3 ½ ounces)

- Salt, kosher (1/4 teaspoon)

- Coconut oil (1 teaspoon)

- Raisins (12 pieces)

- Tomato sauce (14 ½ ounces)

- Duck breasts (2 pieces)

- Turmeric (1 teaspoon)

- Curry leaves (2 stems)

- Cashew nuts, halved (2 pieces)

- Chili powder, Kashmiri (2 teaspoons)

- Garam masala (1/2 teaspoon)

- Onions, caramelized (1/2 cup)

Directions:

1. Trim the fat layers off the duck breasts before scoring the meats. Place in a large bowl and set aside.

2. Place ginger garlic paste (1 teaspoon) in a medium bowl. Add turmeric powder and salt, then stir well to combine. Pour the mixture onto the duck breasts, turning the latter to coat evenly on all sides. Cover and place in the refrigerator to marinate for thirty minutes.

3. Fill the sous vide water oven before preheating to 140 degrees.

4. Remove the marinated duck breasts from the refrigerator and transfer into a large cooking pouch. Vacuum seal before submerging in the preheated sous vide water oven. Allow the duck breasts to cook for

two hours and thirty minutes.

5. Meanwhile, heat a pan (heavy bottomed) on medium before adding the coconut oil. Once the oil is heated through, add the sliced shallots as well as curry leaves; sauté until golden brown.

6. Stir in the raisins, cashew nut, and the rest of the ground spices and ginger garlic paste. Cook for an additional minute before adding in the duck breast. Cook until the surfaces are nicely seared.

7. Pour in the tomato sauce as well as a small amount of water. Stir and allow the mixture to simmer until thickened, before stirring in the salt and coconut milk.

8. Serve the duck meat over a pool of ginger garlic sauce. Top with caramelized onions and enjoy.

10 - Conclusion

Now you know everything there is to know about cooking your food the sous vide way, so any misgivings you may have about giving it a go should be tossed out the kitchen window.

Not sure about the safety of cooking bags or pouches used to hold your ingredients? Rest assured that sous vide plastic containers are made of inert polyethylene material, which means that it does not contain harmful substances like phthalate or BPA that can leach into your "sous videlicious" fares.

You do have to be extra careful with refrigerating your sous vide cooked food. Once you open the pouch, make sure to consume the contents right away or within three days. Sticking your sous vide cooked food in the refrigerator for more than that time frame only gives bacteria the opportunity to flourish and cause you potential harm.

Don't get yourself tied up in choosing the most digitally enhanced sous vide immersion circulator or water oven. The point of cooking with the sous vide method is to be able to cook your food perfectly each and every time after setting your cooking device to your target time and temperature.

Your immersion circulator or water oven can be left alone to work on your food and give you the exact results you want, even if you don't adjust the controls.

Lastly, give yourself a chance to breathe and relax in the knowledge that it is perfectly fine if it takes you several tries before achieving perfection. Once you master the sous vide method of cooking your favorite dishes, eating gourmet quality food at home every day and night of your life is possible.

Book 2 - Sous Vide

Ultimate Low-Temperature Immersion Circulator Guide (Modern Technique, Step-by-Step Instructions, Cooking Through Science)

1 - Introduction

Deceptively Easy

On the outside, it looks intimidating, but the truth is that sous vide cooking is downright simple and achievable. The term "sous vide" is French for "under vacuum" and is used in modern cooking to mean vacuum-sealing your food and then bathing them in warm water for a specific period of time.

This cooking method gives you flavorful food without being overcooked. The food also brims with aromas and juices that make it seem like you are serving up restaurant-quality dishes in the comfort of your home.

Long History

Cooking the sous vide way has a long history of being part of modernist cuisine.

- 1960s: American and French engineers discovered that placing meat inside vacuum bags before cooking them at low temperatures give a more wonderfully textured meat as opposed to cooking it through traditional means.

- 1970s: Top restaurants all over the world started using the sous vide method of cooking to turn out superior quality dishes.

- 1990s: Food scientists performed extensive studies on the sous vide way of cooking food.

- The late 2000s: Sous vide cooking found its way into home kitchens.

- 2008: Thomas Keller, a renowned chef, introduced a guide to the sous vide cooking technique and paved the way for sous vide to be widely used in many U.S. restaurants.

- Present: Both high-end food establishments and home kitchens are serving up meals that are cooked the sous vide way.

Within Reach

The sous vide cooking technique is now more accessible than ever, thanks to immersion circulators that are commercially available in varying sizes, ease of use, and costs. Much of the equipment is handy enough to store inside your kitchen drawer, with some of them being practically a no-brainer with the app-controlled interfaces they come with.

But having a high-tech and ultra-streamlined immersion circulator at your disposal does not mean you have no need of other sous vide equipment. You still need a container to hold your water bath in, a requirement that a twelve-quart cooking pot might easily fill.

But you can choose from plenty of plastic food storage containers that allow you to easily monitor your food as it cooks in the water bath; plus, these commercial food containers possess superior heat retention capabilities.

You also need a vacuum sealer to secure your food in their bags – you can use Ziploc bags if you prefer to cut down on cost, although making use of specially designed plastic bags and securing them with a vacuum sealer allows you to reduce your risk of error and increase your chances of cooking perfect meals.

2 - Sous Videlicious Benefits

The fact that sous vide cooking allows you to accurately control cooking temperatures means that you also get to enjoy these benefits:

You are assured that your food is cooked with consistent doneness from the edges to the center.

You have the opportunity to recreate your meals with near-perfection.

You have greater control on your food's level of doneness, something that is difficult to achieve when cooking through conventional methods.

You can pasteurize your food to make it safe for eating even when cooked at low temperatures (your sous vide steak is safe to eat even when not cooked well-done and your tougher meat cuts can turn out tender even when cooked medium-rare).

You will look forward to getting perfect results each and every time you cook. Cooking chicken breasts, steaks, and other fast-cooking food the sous vide way lets you enjoy the process of cooking itself because you are no longer preoccupied with the usual guesswork that comes with cooking food by traditional means.

When you cook your food using the sous vide technique, thermometer-poking, finger-jabbing, and cutting-and-peeking will now be things of the past.

You enjoy a more flexible schedule that lets you fit in other important tasks. As your immersion circulator quietly heats the bath in which your vacuum-sealed food is submerged in the kitchen, gradually softening your meat until medium-rare and perfectly succulent, you are able to work on your household chores, baby tasks, or exercise routines.

You have the option to pre-cook (long enough to ensure the food is pasteurized) your food (see to it that they are fresh and free from contamination), then chill in the ice bath (for forty-five minutes) before placing in the freezer. Later, you simply reheat, serve, and enjoy eating them.

Know that your sous vide cooked food will always turn out perfectly if you make sure to reheat them below their target cooking temperatures. The one thing you need to keep in mind is the possibility of food contamination, which is why following all the cooking procedures is crucial to guarantee food safety.

(In case there are steps you are not that confident with, it would be best to just eat the sous vide cooked food right away.)

3 - Sous Vide Elements

Sous vide cooking consists of these three elements:

Vacuum sealing

Vacuum sealing your food for sous vide cooking results in the efficient transfer of heat from water bath to your food. This helps in preventing any loss of aromas and juices through evaporation during cooking. Because your ingredients are enclosed in the vacuum-sealed bag along with their accompanying spices/herbs, the latter are able to deliver added flavor in a more intense manner.

Ensuring that your food are vacuum sealed for sous vide cooking also helps in avoiding any off-flavors that might result from the oxidation process (an example would be your meat's fat becoming rancid after long periods of exposure to air).

Moreover, vacuum sealing your sous vide ingredients helps in reducing the risk of re-contaminating them while they are in storage, especially if you are going to cook, store (refrigerate or freeze), and reheat.

Cooking at precise temperatures

Cooking at precise temperatures, an important feature of the sous vide cooking method, allows you to avoid cooking mishaps that can range from turning your should-have-been-perfectly-poached eggs into a single, runny mess, to turning your would-have-been-tender-and-flavorful chicken breast or fish fillet into an ugly, mushy mass.

Cooking at exact times and temperatures also ensures that your food is safe for consumption and helps you figure out its expected shelf life. Because the sous vide cooking method was created with the help of science, you are assured that you will be able to cook your food with perfect timing and with the exact temperature each and every time.

Cooking at low temperatures

At the heart of sous vide cooking is the idea that heat is transferred more effectively through water than through air. This is why you are better off cooking your steak at 135 degrees Fahrenheit in the water bath instead of cooking it at 350 degrees Fahrenheit in a conventional oven.

Besides, cooking at low temperatures lets you turn out more

succulent results. This is because low cooking temperatures do not cause the cell walls in your meat to burst; instead, their connective tissues' tough collagen parts get hydrolyzed into a gelatinous mass.

(In traditional cooking with high temperatures, the same collagen would have been overheated to the point that they are too denatured, resulting in your meat becoming tougher and depleted of moisture, which equals zero flavor.) You can also rest assured that cooking your vegetables at sous vide low temperatures lets you cook them thoroughly and still get that crisp and firm texture you desire.

4 - Sous Vide Prepping Pointers

Preparing your food for cooking the sous vide way is as easy as 1, 2, 3, 4!

Portioning the food

It is best to cut your food into small portions first before cooking with the sous vide method. Doing so ensures that the food reaches the target temperature more quickly and will be cooked through the center.

It is important to see to it that your food gets cooked as quickly as possible, especially when it comes to fish and other extremely tender food – they tend to get mushy when submerged too long in a warm bath.

Another advantage to cutting your food into small portions before sous vide cooking is that you prevent any large areas from being in the dangerous temperature range (40 degrees to 140 degrees Fahrenheit) for long periods, in which micro-bial spoilage can occur.

Seasoning the food

Generously season your food with pepper and salt as well as your preferred spices and herbs.

Bagging and vacuum sealing the food

When cooking large batches of food, or when finding it difficult to place awkwardly-shaped ingredients inside the usual zip-top plastic bags, you can use special vacuum bags that are ideal for sous vide cooking. You can rely on these bags to stand up to tears, leaks, high cooking temperatures, and freezing.

Cooking the food

When cooking your food the sous vide way, you are basically submerging it in the water bath that is preheated to your target temperature. Water is known to be a better conductor of heat than air. Add in the immersion circulator and you are assured that all areas of your water bath is evenly heated.

Cooking your food with the sous vide technique allows you to serve up foods that are evenly cooked through, thanks to the fact that the temperature outside is equal to your target cooking temperature. Another great thing about sous vide cooking is that even if you let your food remain in the bath beyond its targeted time, it will not get overcooked as the temperature will remain constant.

Finishing the food

Once your food is done being sous vide cooked, you can serve it immediately – simply open the vacuum sealed bag, remove the food, and transfer it onto a serving plate. Sous vide cooked foods appear poached when served, which means you can usually serve eggs, skinless poultry meats, fish, and shellfish as is.

As for other meats like steak, lamb, and pork, these are not usually served poached, so you can make them look even more palatable by searing after cooking.

A great steak is usually characterized by a wonderfully browned and seared surface. Most of the steak's flavor comes from this tasty, crispy skin, something that you can get only if you subject it to high temperatures. Now, sous vide cooking is all about cooking your food at low temperature, so it is important to sear the food afterwards to make sure it develops that much desired browned taste.

You may use a blowtorch to sear smaller cuts of meat. A blowtorch's high heat effectively sears food surfaces while leaving the interior of the sliced parts alone. To prevent any unpleasant aromas that might result from searing your food with a blowtorch, make sure to use the recommended MAPP (methylacetylene propadiene propene) gas.

If searing flat sous vide cooked foods, there is always the pan or griddle to help you. You can sear chicken, pork, or beef in a pan made of cast iron, and fish, scallops, and other more delicate foods in a pan made of stainless steel.

To get the temperature transfer going at a faster rate, you can grease the pan first with a high smoke point oil like sunflower oil or canola oil. Heat the pan before adding about a tablespoon of oil (just enough to coat the entire pan's bottom). Once the oil is hot, smoking, and starting to brown, add the sous vide cooked meat (pat-dried with paper towels).

You may also use an extremely hot grill to give your sous vide cooked foods those desired grill marks.

If you wish to deep fry your sous vide cooked foods for a deeply browned and crispier exterior, try dipping them first in liquid nitrogen; this will help keep the foods from being overcooked as they are deep-fried.

5 - Quick Guide to Sous Vide Tools

Things to Consider

Temperature stability

Any change in temperature by as much as one degree makes a huge difference to how your sous vide cooked food turns out. Make sure to use are using a sous vide tool that possesses a ± 32 degrees Fahrenheit temperature stability. Due to its water pumps and other electronics, using an immersion circulator will ensure that the water in your bath is circulated properly.

Water bath container

Choose a water bath container that is specially manufactured for use in sous vide cooking. This will assure you of excellent insulation for less energy consumption as well as reduced water evaporation, which are crucial when cooking your food for more than eighteen hours.

Water bath capacity

You can choose water bath containers with capacities that range from 5 liters to 120 liters. The important thing to remember is that you have to have adequate free space between all food bags you place inside the water bath – this is to ensure that the water can circulate well. Make sure not to fill more than ½ of the water bath container with food bags.

Heating power

The heating power of your immersion circulator determines the time it takes to heat up your water bath to reach the target temperature before cooking the food.

Size of equipment

Immersion circulators are handy and take up only a small space in your kitchen. You can even store them standing up on the counter, which is great for keeping your kitchen clutter-free and organized-looking.

Maintenance and cleaning

Make sure to choose sous vide tools that are easy to clean, easy to maintain, have no exposed parts to cause you harm, and if possible, coated with nonstick surfaces.

Safety

One concern with sous vide cooking is the fact that you are dealing with evaporating water. This is the reason you need to make sure that your sous vide cooking bags are properly and constantly submerged in the heated water bath. Look for a device that has a lid to ensure decreased water evaporation.

You might also try a device that comes with an alarm that gets triggered whenever the water level measuring part of the device detects an extremely low water level. It would also be best to make sure that your immersion circulator comes with a protective shield for helping keep the sous vide bags away from the pump and heating coil.

6 - Essentials to Have

Aside from sous vide cooking bags to place your food in, you need the following:

Immersion circulator

An immersion circulator comes with motors that heat the water in your bath, and then circulate it inside the container. This is what keeps the temperature of the water constant and evenly distributed, both of which are important in sous vide cooking.

What is great about using an immersion circulator is that you can use it with different sizes of cooking pots. This device is also small enough to be easily stored, always a plus when choosing any kitchen device.

Vacuum sealer (chamber vacuum packer)

A chamber vacuum packer or sealer lets you seal your sous vide food bags with ease and peace of mind. Simply position the whole cooking bag inside the inner chamber of the machine. Close the lid and allow the packer to extract the air inside the chamber, which forces out the air from inside the bag.

Thermometer

A thermometer of good quality, when used with a special foam tape, is useful in monitoring your food's temperature once it is placed in the sous vide bag. This is important because it gives you an idea of when your food will reach its target temperature for cooking perfectly.

7 - Tips on Sous Vide Target Times and Temperatures

Steak: T-Bone/Porterhouse, Ribeye, Butcher's Cuts, and Strip

The following timings are provided for steaks cut that are about 1½-inches to 2-inches thick. If cooking steaks with a thickness of 1-inch or less, you can shorten the initial cooking time to forty minutes. For steaks that are sous vide cooked at less than 130 degrees Fahrenheit, make sure to cook them for no more than 2½ hours to keep them safe for consumption.

Very rare/Rare doneness

- Temperature range – 120 degrees Fahrenheit to 128 degrees Fahrenheit

- Timing range – 1 hour to 2 hours

Medium to rare doneness

- Temperature range – 129 degrees Fahrenheit to 134 degrees Fahrenheit

- Timing range – 1 hour to 4 hours (if under 130 degrees Fahrenheit, it should be 2 ½ hours maximum)

Medium doneness

- Temperature range – 135 degrees Fahrenheit to 144 degrees Fahrenheit

- Timing range – 1 hour to 4 hours

Medium to well-done

- Temperature range – 145 degrees Fahrenheit to 155 degrees Fahrenheit

- Timing range – 1 hour to 3 ½ hours

Well-done

- Temperature range – 156 degrees Fahrenheit and up

- Timing range – 1 hour to 3 hours

Steak: Tenderloin

It is easy to overcook lean tenderloin and have it end up dry because of the absence of intramuscular fat in this cut of meat. To avoid this dilemma, consider cooking your tender-loin at a temperature that is several Fahrenheit degrees lower than ribeye, strip, and other fattier meat cuts.

You might also try sous vide cooking your tenderloin between very rare and rare (within 120 degrees Fahrenheit and 128 degrees Fahrenheit) to ensure that it is tenderly cooked and retains its juiciness.

The following timings are for steaks that are about 1 ½ to 2 inches in thickness. If cooking steaks with 1 inch or less thickness, simply decrease the initial cooking time to thirty minutes. If cooking steaks below 130 degrees Fahrenheit, see to it that you cook it for more than 2 ½ hours to ensure food safety.

Very rare/Rare doneness

- Temperature range – 120 degrees Fahrenheit to 128 degrees Fahrenheit

- Timing range – 45 minutes to 2 ½ hours

Medium to rare doneness

- Temperature range – 129 degrees Fahrenheit to 134 degrees Fahrenheit

- Timing range – 45 minutes to 4 hours (if under 130

degrees Fahrenheit, it should be 2 ½ hours maximum)

Medium doneness

- Temperature range – 135 degrees Fahrenheit to 144 degrees Fahrenheit

- Timing range – 45 minutes to 4 hours

Medium to well-done

- Temperature range – 145 degrees Fahrenheit to 155 degrees Fahrenheit

- Timing range – 45 minutes to 3 ½ hours

Well-done

- Temperature range – 156 degrees Fahrenheit and up

- Timing range – 1 hour to 3 hours

Chicken Breast

Tender and juicy – great for using in cold chicken salads

- Temperature range – 150 degrees Fahrenheit

- Timing range – 1 hour to 4 hours

Juicy and very soft – best served hot

- Temperature range – 140 degrees Fahrenheit

- Timing range – 1 ½ hours to 4 hours

Slightly stringy, tender, and juicy – best served hot

- Temperature range – 150 degrees Fahrenheit

- Timing range – 1 hour to 4 hours

Slightly stringy, traditional, firm, and juicy – best served hot

- Temperature range – 160 degrees Fahrenheit

- Timing range – 1 hour to 4 hours

Shrimp

Translucent, semi-raw, and with buttery, soft texture

- Temperature range – 125 degrees Fahrenheit

- Timing range – 15 minutes

Nearly opaque, slightly firm, very tender

- Temperature range – 130 degrees Fahrenheit

- Timing range – 15 minutes

Barely opaque, juicy, tender, and moist

- Temperature range – 135 degrees Fahrenheit

- Timing range – 15 minutes

Poached texture, traditional, juicy, with good bounce, and with snappy bite

- Temperature range – 140 degrees Fahrenheit

- Timing range – 15 minutes

Lobster

Translucent and soft

- Temperature range – 120 degrees Fahrenheit

- Timing range – 20 minutes

Succulent and tender

- Temperature range – 130 degrees Fahrenheit

- Timing range – 30 minutes to 45 minutes

Traditional, with steamed lobster texture

- Temperature range – 140 degrees Fahrenheit

- Timing range – 1 hour

Halibut

Tender, just about to flake, and with near-raw layers

- Temperature range – 125 degrees Fahrenheit

- Timing range – 45 minutes for 1-inch thick fillets; 45 minutes to 1 hour for up to 2-inches thick fillets

Tender, flaky, and extremely moist

- Temperature range – 130 degrees Fahrenheit

- Timing range – 45 minutes for 1-inch thick fillets; 45 minutes to 1 hour for up to 2-inches thick fillets

Firm, flaky, moist, and about to develop a tough texture

- Temperature range – 140 degrees Fahrenheit

- Timing range – 45 minutes for 1-inch thick fillets; 45 minutes to 1 hour for up to 2-inches thick fillets

Tuna

Rare/nearly raw, slightly firm, to be served chilled

- Temperature range – 105 degrees Fahrenheit

- Timing range – 45 minutes for 1-inch thick fillets; 45 minutes to 1 hour for up to 2-inches thick fillets

Just firmed and extremely moist

- Temperature range – 110 degrees Fahrenheit

- Timing range – 45 minutes for 1-inch thick fillets; 45 minutes to 1 hour for up to 2-inches thick fillets

Moist and meaty

- Temperature range – 115 degrees Fahrenheit

- Timing range – 45 minutes for 1-inch thick fillets; 45 minutes to 1 hour for up to 2-inches thick fillets

Dry, firm, and with well-done steak texture

- Temperature range – 120 degrees Fahrenheit

- Timing range – 45 minutes for 1-inch thick fillets; 45 minutes to 1 hour for up to 2-inches thick fillets

Firm, crumbly, dry, and to be used in recipes calling for canned tuna

- Temperature range – 130 degrees Fahrenheit

- Timing range – 45 minutes for 1-inch thick fillets; 45 minutes to 1 hour for up to 2-inches thick fillets

Lamb

Very rare/rare doneness

- Temperature range – 115 degrees Fahrenheit to 124 degrees Fahrenheit

- Timing range – 1 hour to 4 hours (if cooking under 130 degrees Fahrenheit, it should be 2 ½ hours maximum)

Medium to rare doneness

- Temperature range – 125 degrees Fahrenheit to 134

degrees Fahrenheit

- Timing range – 45 minutes to 4 hours (if cooking under 130 degrees Fahrenheit, it should be 2 ½ hours maximum)

Medium doneness

- Temperature range – 135 degrees Fahrenheit to 144 degrees Fahrenheit

- Timing range – 1 hour to 4 hours

Medium to well-done

- Temperature range – 145 degrees Fahrenheit to 154 degrees Fahrenheit

- Timing range – 1 hour to 4 hours

Well-done

- Temperature range – 155 degrees Fahrenheit and up

- Timing range – 1 hour to 4 hours

Turkey

Very pink, extra moist, and soft

- Temperature range – 132 degrees Fahrenheit / 130 degrees Fahrenheit

- Timing range – 2 hours / 4 hours

Pale pink, moist, and soft

- Temperature range – 138 degrees Fahrenheit / 136 degrees Fahrenheit

- Timing range – 1 hour / 3 hours

White, moist, and tender

- Temperature range – 145 degrees Fahrenheit / 143 degrees Fahrenheit

- Timing range – 16 minutes / 2 ½ hours

White, with traditional roasted texture

- Temperature range – 152 degrees Fahrenheit / 150 degrees Fahrenheit

- Timing range – 4 minutes / 2 hours

8 - Guide to Sous Vide Cooking Steak

Step-by-Step Instructions for Sous Vide Cooking Steak:

1. Set the sous vide cooker to the target temperature to preheat. Add the steak only once the desired temperature is reached by the water bath.

2. Sprinkle the steak generously with pepper and salt, making sure the edges are seasoned as well, before placing in the cooking pouch or bag.

3. Add in any aromatics you want to use in your steak, such as sprigs of rosemary or thyme. See to it that they are evenly distributed on both surfaces of the seasoned steak.

4. Seal the cooking bag using a vacuum sealer or through the displacement method (if cooking your steak in a bag with a zipper-lock). If using the displacement method, gradually lower the cooking bag into a pot filled with water, then allow water pressure to press out the air inside the bag through its top. Securely seal the bag over the waterline as soon as most

of the air pockets are released.

5. Place the steak bag in the preheated water bath and allow it to sink. Follow the correct timing in cooking the steak.

6. Once the steak is done, remove the cooking bag out of the sous vide cooker. Take the steak out of the bag and transfer onto a plate lined with paper towels. To dry, carefully pat on both sides.

Step-by-Step Instructions for Finishing the Sous Vide Cooked Steak (Stovetop):

1. Heat a large cast iron skillet (heavy bottomed) over high heat. Add the vegetable oil (1 tablespoon), turning the skillet to spread the oil evenly.

2. Once the oil is heated through and is beginning to smoke, add the steak as well as butter (1 tablespoon), if preferred, to help the steak develop a dark crust and slightly charred taste.

3. Add whole sprigs of rosemary and thyme to the pan, as well as crushed garlic cloves and sliced shallots.

4. Allow the steak to cook for fifteen to thirty seconds on one side, then flip it every fifteen seconds thereafter in the next one minutes and thirty seconds or until nicely browned and seared. If you skipped the butter earlier, add it to the pan about half a minute before the steak is cooked.

5. Give your sous vide steak that steakhouse-quality char by flaming with a torch (high output). Avoid any off-aromas from the torched steak by making sure to simultaneously heat it in the skillet. Use slow and even strokes in torching on one side, making sure to apply the torch flame back and forth on the surface. Once the meat turns pale brown and shows several singed spots, flip to torch on the other side.

6. Use tongs to hold the steak by the edges. Rotate the meat on its edges as you cook it for an additional forty-five seconds or until all edges are browned.

7. Set a wire rack inside a baking sheet (rimmed). Once the steak is done, transfer to the rack and allow it to rest.

8. Serve the steak drenched in reheated pan juices and

fat.

Step-by-Step Instructions for Finishing the Sous Vide Cooked Steak (Grill):

1. Finishing your sous vide cooked steak on the grill will be a breeze if you do it outside. Place the cooked steak inside a cooler and bring outside.

2. Fill a chimney with lots of charcoal. Light the charcoal and allow it to burn until covered with ash. Discard the ash and set the coals to one corner of the grate. After setting the cooking grate into place, cover the grill and preheat for about five minutes.

3. Add the steak directly on top of the grill's hot side. Cook for about one minute and thirty seconds or until deeply crusted on the surface (make sure to turn the steak every fifteen to thirty seconds).

4. Once the steak is done, place on a platter. Serve and enjoy.

9 - Recipe Using Sous Vide Cooked Steak:

Salsa Verde Steak with Corn Salad

Ingredients:

Salsa verde:

- Cornichons, minced finely (8 pieces)

- Anchovy fillets, roughly minced (6 pieces)

- Olive oil, extra virgin (1/2 cup)

- Parsley leaves, fresh, minced (1 cup + 1 tablespoon)

- Dijon mustard (2 teaspoons)

- Sherry vinegar (2 tablespoons)

- Capers, drained, minced finely (2 tablespoons)

- Garlic cloves, medium, minced (2 pieces)

- Mint leaves, fresh, minced (1/2 cup + 1/2 tablespoon)

- Shallot, small, minced (2 tablespoons)

- Salt, kosher (1/2 teaspoon)

- Black pepper, freshly ground (1/2 teaspoon)

Salad:

- Steak, sous vide cooked, pan-seared, chilled, sliced thinly (3/4 pound)

- Corn ears, in husk (2 pieces)

- Red onion, sliced thinly (1 piece)

Directions:

1. Pour the sherry vinegar into a large mixing bowl. Add the anchovies, cornichons, parsley, shallot, capers, garlic, mint, and mustard. Whisk well to combine before drizzling in the olive oil. Season with pepper and salt; let sit.

2. Meanwhile, shuck the corn before grilling under the broiler or on top of a heated grill. Make sure to turn the corn frequently as it cooks for eight minutes or until tender and a bit charred. (You may also put the shucked corn on a plate (microwave safe) and microwave it for about seven minutes or until tender and steamed through.) Once the corn is done, let sit until slightly cooled and then cut off its kernels.

3. Discard the corn cobs, then place the corn kernels in a large mixing bowl. Add the red onion as well as steak and salsa verde (1/2 cup), then toss to combine. Season with pepper and salt before transferring the steak mixture onto a platter. Pour on some extra salsa verde and then top with mint and parsley leaves.

4. Serve right away.

5. Enjoy.

10 - Guide to Sous Vide Cooking Lamb

Step-by-Step Instructions for Sous Vide Cooking a Lamb Rack:

1. Set the sous vide cooker to your target temperature to preheat. (Once that temperature is reached, you can then add the lamb rack.)

2. Liberally season all sides of the lamb rack with pepper and salt.

3. Place the seasoned lamb rack inside the sous vide bag before vacuum sealing.

4. Submerge the lamb rack bag into the preheated water bath to cook.

5. Take the sous vide cooked lamb rack out of the bag and transfer onto a plate lined with paper towels. Carefully pat it dry on each side.

6. Heat a stainless steel/ cast iron skillet (heavy bottomed) on high, then add vegetable oil/ rice bran oil/ canola oil (1 tablespoon). Once the oil is smoking, add the lamb rack with the bones facing up and making

sure that the skillet is not crowded. To avoid this, consider cooking in batches.

7. Heat a cast iron skillet on medium-high. Add butter (1 tablespoon); once melted, add garlic cloves and shallot (roughly chopped) or whole sprigs of rosemary or thyme. Add the lamb and toss in the skillet so that all sides are evenly seared. Spoon the butter onto the lamb to baste it as it cooks for one minute. Turn the lamb to its other side and cook for an additional minute, making sure to baste it with butter as well.

8. Once the lamb is done, transfer to a cutting board. Use a sharp knife to slice down the ribs.

9. Serve smothered with the juices and fat left in the skillet.

Recipe Using Sous Vide Cooked Lamb:

Black Mustard and Mint Leg of Lamb

Ingredients:

- Black mustard seeds, whole (1 tablespoon)

- Mint leaves, fresh, chopped finely (1 ounce)

- Chili, red jalapeno/ Fresno, minced finely (1 piece)

- Salt, kosher (1/4 teaspoon)

- Black pepper, freshly ground (1/4 teaspoon)

- Shallot, small, minced (1 piece)

- Olive oil, extra virgin (3 tablespoons)

- Vegetable oil, divided (3 tablespoons)

- Cumin seeds, whole (2 teaspoons)

- Leg of lamb, boneless, butterflied, 5-pounds (1/2 piece)

- Cilantro leaves, fresh, w/ intact tender steams, chopped finely (1 ounce)

- Garlic clove, medium, minced finely (1 piece)

- Red wine vinegar (1 tablespoon)

Directions:

1. Heat a small skillet on medium-high, then add in the vegetable oil (2 tablespoons). Allow the oil to heat

through and shimmer before stirring in the cumin as well as the mustard. Cook for about half a minute or until fragrant; once done, pour right away into a large bowl (heat-proof), sprinkle with pepper and salt, and set aside to cool.

2. Take ½ portion of the cooled spice mixture and rub on the lamb leg's interior side. Roll back up and secure with a kitchen twine, making sure to tie from each end of the leg and working your way toward the middle at one-inch intervals. Season with additional pepper and salt before setting aside on a tray.

3. Meanwhile, set the water bath to the target temperature to preheat. Place the rolled lamb leg inside a sous vide bag, vacuum seal, and submerge in the water bath to cook until tenderly done.

4. Place the mustard-cumin mixture in a large bowl. Add the red wine vinegar as well as olive oil, garlic, cilantro, chili, mint, and shallot. Stir well to combine before adding in pepper and salt; let the chimichurri sit.

5. Once the lamb is done, remove from the sous vide

bag and transfer onto a large plate lined with paper towels. Pat dry carefully and set aside.

6. Heat a large skillet (cast iron) on medium before adding in vegetable oil (1 tablespoon). Once the oil is lightly smoking, add the sous vide cooked lamb and cook for about four minutes or until all of its sides are nicely browned.

7. Untie the twine off the lamb. Slice, serve and enjoy the prepared chimichurri.

11 - Guide to Sous Vide Cooking Chicken Breast

Step-by-Step Instructions for Sous Vide Cooking a Chicken Breast:

1. Set the sous vide cooker to your target temperature.

2. Place the chicken breasts (skin on, bone in) in a large bowl. Season well with pepper and salt before transferring to a sous vide bag.

3. Add fresh herbs and/or sliced lemons to the chicken bag, then vacuum seal.

4. Submerge the chicken bag into the preheated sous vide cooker. Allow it to sink and then cook until perfectly done.

Step-by-Step Instructions for Finishing the Sous Vide Cooked Chicken

1. Take the cooked chicken out of the sous vide bag. After discarding any aromatics you may have included, transfer the chicken to a plate lined with paper towels. Gently pat dry the meat on both sides to

remove excess moisture. Set aside.

2. Meanwhile, heat a skillet (cast iron) on medium-high. Add oil (vegetable/rice bran/canola), spreading evenly to coat the pan. Once the oil is shimmering hot, add the chicken, making sure its skin is facing down.

3. Cook the chicken for about two minutes or until its skin is nicely seared, crisp, and browned. Turn off the heat and let the seared chicken sit for two minutes or until slightly cooled.

4. Carefully pull out the wishbone before separating the breast meat from the breastbone.

5. Slice the chicken into four equal sized portions.

6. Serve topped with your favorite sauce, homemade vinaigrette, or lemon wedges drizzled with olive oil.

Step-by-Step Instructions for Finishing the Sous Vide Cooked Chicken Breast (Grill):

1. Take out the sous vide cooked chicken out of the bag.

Place on a plate lined with paper towels after removing any aromatics used.

2. Carefully pat the chicken with the paper towels to dry before letting it sit to cool for about two minutes or until you are finished preheating the grill.

3. Fill the chimney (half) with plenty of charcoal. Allow all charcoal to get lit before covering with gray ash and dragging the coals to the charcoal grate. Arrange the charcoal on one side before positioning the cooking grate. After covering the grill, preheat for about five minutes.

4. Making sure its skin is facing down, add the chicken to the grill and allow to cook for about four to five minutes or until crisp and brown on all sides. Transfer onto a plate and allow to cool for two minutes before removing the bones.

5. Carve the seared chicken and serve immediately.

6. Enjoy.

Recipe Using Sous Vide Cooked Chicken Breast:

Easy Chicken Salad

Ingredients:

- Lemons, whole (2 pieces)

- Parsley leaves, fresh, minced (1 tablespoon)

- Celery, diced finely (1/2 cup)

- Mayonnaise, homemade (1/4 cup + 1 tablespoon)

- Red onion, diced finely (1/2 cup)

- Dijon mustard (1 tablespoon + 1 teaspoon)

- Chives, fresh, minced (1 tablespoon)

- Salt, kosher (1/2 teaspoon)

- Black pepper, freshly ground (1/2 teaspoon)

- Tarragon sprigs, whole (4 pieces) + tarragon leaves, fresh, minced, divided (1 tablespoon)

- Garlic clove, medium, minced (1 piece)

- Chicken breast, whole, skin on, bone in, split into halves (1 ¾ pounds)

Directions:

1. Set the sous vide cooker at 150 degrees to preheat.

2. Sprinkle pepper and salt liberally on the chicken to season well. Place inside a sous vide bag and top with lemon slices (cut the 2 whole lemons into quarter-inch slices) and whole sprigs of tarragon.

3. Vacuum seal the chicken bag and place in the sous vide cooker to cook for one to four hours. Once done, transfer the chicken bag into an ice bath; set aside to chill for about fifteen minutes. (Alternatively, you can heat a large saucepot (heavy bottomed) filled with two quarts worth of water on medium-high until it reaches 155 degrees. Once the target water temperature is reached, pour the water into a cooler. Add the chicken-filled sous vide bag before sealing the cooler, then allow the chicken to cook for one to four hours, adding more boiling water as needed to keep the water temperature at 150 degrees. Once done, place the chicken bag in an ice bath and allow to chill for fifteen minutes.)

4. Combine the lemon juice (2 tablespoons) and lemon

zest (1 teaspoon) in a large bowl. Stir in the chives, minced tarragon leaves, celery, parsley, garlic, red onion, mustard, and mayonnaise. Once well-mixed, place in the refrigerator.

5. Once the sous vide cooked chicken has cooled, remove from the bag. Take out the lemon slices and tarragon stems and discard.

6. Transfer the chicken to a plate. Slice into half-inch chunks and place inside the bowl containing the mayonnaise mixture. Gently fold in the chicken chunks as you sprinkle on pepper and salt.

7. Serve your dresses sous vide chicken breast on a bed of lettuce.

8. Enjoy.

12 - Guide to Sous Vide Cooking Pulled Pork Shoulder

Step-by-Step Instructions for Sous Vide Cooking Pulled Pork Shoulder:

1. Fill the spice grinder with the mustard seed and brown sugar. Add the salt, black pepper, paprika, red pepper flakes, oregano, garlic powder, and coriander seed. Grind the ingredients until combined and reduced to a powdered mix (do this batches).

2. You might consider adding in pink curing salt (1/4 teaspoon) to the spice mixture if you prefer having a pinkish smoke ring on the pork shoulder. Reserve 3 tablespoons of your spice mix (to be used later in seasoning the meat before finishing), generously rub all over the meat to season it well.

3. Transfer the seasoned pork shoulder into a sous vide bag. Keep the seal of the sous vide bag from weakening by folding it over as you add the meat to make sure no trace of the spice mix rubs on the bag's edge. If preferred, pour in some liquid smoke (1/2 teaspoon) before vacuum sealing the bag.

4. Meanwhile, set the sous vide cooker at 165 degrees to preheat if you want your pork shoulder easy to pull apart. (If you would like your meat to be tender but sliceable, set the cooker at 145 degrees.)

5. Submerge the pork shoulder bag into the preheated water bath. Allow the meat to cook for about eighteen to twenty-four hours. Consider tenting the container with plastic wrap or aluminum foil to keep the circulator shut down due to excessive evaporation.

6. Once the sous vide pork shoulder is done, remove from the water bath. Place the pork shoulder bag in the refrigerator to chill for up to seven days if not serving right away.

7. Give the pork shoulder meat another good rub with the spice mix. This will give the meat that desired flavorful, dark, and crunchy bark after you finish it.

Step-by-Step Instructions for Finishing the Sous Vide Cooked Pulled Pork Shoulder (Smoker):

1. After lighting up the smoker, set to 300 degrees to preheat.

2. Fill with un-soaked hardwood. Once it smolders, add the sous vide cooked pork shoulder and cook for two hours and thirty minutes or until the meat can be easily pulled apart and a dark mahogany crust has developed on the surface.

Step-by-Step Instructions for Finishing the Sous Vide Cooked Pulled Pork Shoulder (Oven):

1. Set the oven to 300 degrees to preheat.

2. Place a wire rack inside a baking sheet (rimmed) lined with foil. Set the pork on the rack and place in the oven to cook for one hour and thirty minutes or until the surface develops a dark mahogany crust. Once done, take the pork shoulder out of the oven

and transfer onto a platter.

3. Use two forks or your fingers (protected by thick plastic gloves) pull the meat. Shred into chunky cuts or chop on the cutting board afterward for finer shreds.

4. Pour your favorite sauce on the pulled meat and serve right away with a soft bun and a small mound of creamy coleslaw.

Recipe Using Sous Vide Cooked Pulled Pork Shoulder:

Spicy Pulled Pork with Chorizo and Corn Slaw

Ingredients:

Pulled pork:

- Ancho chili powder (2 tablespoons)

- Black pepper, freshly ground (1/2 teaspoon)

- Cloves, ground (1/8 teaspoon)

- Garlic cloves, medium, minced (5 pieces)

- Vinegar, apple cider (2 tablespoons + 1 teaspoon)

- Cumin, ground (2 teaspoons)

- Cinnamon, ground (1/4 teaspoon)

- Oil, vegetable/ canola (2 tablespoons)

- Cornstarch (2 tablespoons)

- Yellow onion, medium, diced (1 piece)

- Amber lager, Mexican (24 ounces)

- Paprika (2 tablespoons)

- Salt, kosher (2 tablespoons)

- Coriander, ground (1/4 teaspoon)

- Pork shoulder, boneless, sliced into three-inch cubes (3 ½ pounds)

- Oregano, Mexican, dried (1 teaspoon)

- Cayenne pepper, ground (1/2 teaspoon)

- Tortillas/ burger buns (8 pieces)

Corn slaw:

- Green cabbage, shredded finely (14 ounces)

- Cotija cheese, crumbled (3 ounces)

- Honey (1 tablespoon)

- Jalapeno peppers, seeded, minced (1 piece)

- Lime juice, freshly squeezed (2 tablespoons)

- Mayonnaise, homemade (1/4 cup)

- Corn kernels, fresh cooked (2 cups)

- Garlic cloves, medium, minced (2 pieces)

- Ancho chili powder (1 tablespoon)

- Cilantro leaves, fresh, w/ intact tender stems, chopped (1/2 cup)

- Salt, kosher (1/4 teaspoon)

Directions:

1. Place all ingredients for making the corn slaw in a large bowl. Gently toss to combine, cover, and place

in the refrigerator to chill before using later.

2. Fill a medium bowl with the ground peppers as well as cloves, salt, oregano, cinnamon, paprika, cumin, coriander, and chili powder. Stir to combine and rub on all sides of the pork. Transfer the coated pork in a large bowl, cover, and place in the refrigerator to chill overnight.

3. Set the oven to 300 degrees to preheat. Meanwhile, heat a Dutch oven on medium-high before adding in the oil. Once lightly smoking, add the pork and cook (in batches) for eight minutes or until all sides are nicely browned. Once done, place the pork on a large plate.

4. Reheat the same skillet on medium. Add the onions to cook for about three minutes or until softened a bit. Stir in the garlic and cook for an additional minute.

5. Add the browned pork back to the pot. Add the beer, then allow the mixture to boil before covering and transferring to the preheated oven. Cook for about three hours or until you can easily shred the meat us-

ing two forks.

6. Once the pork is done in the oven, remove and strain (set the liquid aside in a small bowl). Transfer the pork to a large plate and shred before setting aside.

7. Meanwhile, add the reserve liquid back to the pot. Allow it to boil on medium-high before reducing heat to low and allowing it to simmer.

8. Mix water (3 tablespoons) to the cornstarch before adding to the simmering liquid in the pot. Allow the mixture to simmer for several minutes more to thicken before adding in apple cider vinegar. Add the shredded pork as well and stir to combine.

9. Place the shredded pork on warmed buns and serve with the prepared corn slaw.

13 - Guide to Sous Vide Cooking Shrimp

Step-by-Step Instructions for Sous Vide Cooking Shrimp:

1. Heat a skillet (cast iron) on low. Add olive oil (2 tablespoons) and garlic slices (2 cloves). Cook until the garlic is fragrant and tender, then stir in dried bay leaves (2 pieces) as well as smoked paprika (a pinch).

2. Once the mixture gives off a toasty paprika aroma, pour in sherry (a splash) as well as sherry vinegar (2 tablespoons). Stir to combine as you add butter (2 slices) as well.

3. Set the sous vide cooker to your target temperature to preheat.

4. Fill a sous vide bag with the shrimps. Add the flavored oil, vacuum seal, and lower into the preheated water bath. Cook for fifteen to thirty minutes or until the shrimp are plump.

5. Once done, transfer onto a platter and serve right away.

Recipe Using Sous Vide Cooked Shrimp:

Green Apple and Spicy Shrimp Salad

Ingredients:

- Water, filtered (2 quarts)

- Apples, Granny Smith, large (2 pieces)

- Cashews, plain, roasted, unsalted (1 ½ cups)

- Tomatoes, on the vine, medium (3 pieces)

- Lime juice, freshly squeezed (1 tablespoon)

- Mint leaves, fresh, torn into bits (1/3 cup)

- Shrimp, large, peeled, deveined (1 ½ pounds)

- Salt, kosher (2 tablespoons)

- Shallots, large (2 pieces) OR red onion, large (1/2 piece)

- Red pepper flakes, dried (1/4 teaspoon)

- Fish sauce, reduced sodium (1 teaspoon)

Directions:

1. Fill a large pot with water and heat on medium-high. Add salt and allow the water to boil. Once boiling, turn heat down to medium so that the boiling water is merely steaming. Use a thermometer to ensure that the water maintains a temperature between 160 and 180 degrees (the ideal temperature range needed to poach shrimp).

2. Add the shrimp to the steaming water. Stir continuously and cook for one minute or until the shrimp flesh is opaque. Once done, transfer into a colander to drain set aside in a large bowl.

3. Cut off the tops from the tomatoes before slicing them into half-inch wedged portions. Toss into the bowl containing the poached shrimp.

4. Remove the peel from the red onion, then cut into thin lengthwise slices. Toss into the shrimp bowl as well.

5. After coring the apples, slice into halves before slicing again into 1/8-inch portions. Carefully stack the apple slices and slice again to form 1/8-inch thick matchsticks, then toss into the shrimp bowl.

6. Add the red pepper flakes as well as lime juice and fish sauce. Toss gently to combine all ingredients, making sure the chicken chunks are evenly coated.

7. Toss in the mint leaves and cashews. Serve alone or with a small mound of freshly steamed rice. Enjoy.

14 - Guide to Sous Vide Cooking Halibut

Step-by-Step Instructions for Sous Vide Cooking Halibut:

1. Sprinkle generous amounts of pepper and salt on the halibut fillets (4 pieces) to season them well.

2. Place the seasoned halibut fillets inside a sous vide bag along with butter (4 teaspoons). Make sure the fillets are aligned to form a single layer. Include dill, parsley, thyme, or other aromatic herbs (you might also try adding grated citrus zest or thin shallot slices instead). Avoid putting any acidic ingredient in the bag to prevent altering the fish texture, or any chunky ingredient that may damage the fillet shapes.

3. Vacuum seal the bag to close and place in the refrigerator to rest for half an hour or overnight. This will help dry-brine and firm up the fish flesh to improve its texture and flavor.

4. Set the sous vide cooker to your target temperature.

5. Take the halibut fillets out of the refrigerator and

submerge into the water bath. Allow the fish to cook for about thirty to forty-five minutes (if you are using 1-inch-thick halibut fillets) or for forty-five minutes to one hour (if you are using 2-inch-thick halibut fillets).

6. Once the halibut fillets are done, take out of the sous vide bag and transfer onto sheets of paper towels. Take another paper towel and use to gently blot each fillet on top.

7. Remove the aromatic herbs and halibut skin to discard, then serve immediately.

8. Step-by-Step Instructions for Finishing the Sous Vide Cooked Halibut (Searing):

9. Heat a large skillet (heavy bottomed) on medium-high before adding butter (1 tablespoon). Once the butter is foaming hot, add the sous vide cooked halibut fillets and on one side for about thirty to forty-five seconds or until a bit browned.

10. Add garlic, thyme, shallots, and other aromatics to the skillet. Cook in the hot butter and use the mixture to baste the fillets. After one minute and thirty

seconds or once the halibut fillets are browned through, flip to cook on the other side for an additional fifteen to thirty seconds.

11. Drain off excess oil from the halibut fillets by placing on several sheets of paper towels. Transfer to a platter and serve.

Recipe Using Sous Vide Cooked Halibut:

Dill Halibut and Clams

Ingredients:

- Yellow onion, medium, diced (1 piece)

- White wine, dry (1 cup)

- Halibut fillets, skinless, sous vide cooked, 6-ounces (4 pieces)

- Clams, littleneck, scrubbed (12 pieces)

- Garlic cloves, medium, chopped roughly (2 pieces)

- Dill, chopped (1 tablespoon)

- Butter, unsalted, divided (4 tablespoons)

- Fennel bulb, small, halved, cored, diced (1 piece + a handful of fronds)

- Celery stalk, diced (1 piece)

- Water, filtered (2 cups)

- Salt, kosher (1/2 teaspoon)

- Black pepper, freshly ground (1/2 teaspoon)

Directions:

1. Heat a large sauté pan (straight sided) on medium-high. Add butter (2 tablespoons) and allow to melt and foam before stirring in the onion, garlic, celery, and diced fennel. Cook for about three minutes or until the vegetables are softened.

2. Pour in the wine, stir, and cook for four minutes or until the mixture is reduced to ½ its original volume. Add water as well as the sous vide cooked halibut fillets (seasoned with pepper and salt), making sure the fillets are partially submerged in cooking liquid. Surround the fillets with the clams and continue cooking until the mixture simmers. Cover and reduce heat before cooking for an additional five minutes or until

the fillets are completely cooked and the clams are open.

3. Place the halibut fillets and clams in individual bowls. Add the vegetables and set aside.

4. Meanwhile, pour broth into a pot. Add butter and dill, then whisk to combine. Once the butter is completely melted into the mixture and the broth is heated through, season with pepper and salt.

5. Pour the broth into the bowls filled with halibut and clams. Serve garnished with fennel fronds or parsley.

6. Enjoy.

15 - Guide to Sous Vide Cooking Turkey

Step-by-Step Instructions for Sous Vide Cooking Extra Crispy-Skinned Turkey Breast:

1. Take the whole turkey breast and set on a cutting board. Remove the skin, making sure to take the entire skin in one go.

2. Separate the breastbone from the breast halves by using a sharp-edged boning knife. You can set the breastbone aside for making gravy later.

3. Sprinkle liberal amounts of pepper and salt on the bottom sides of the turkey breast halves to season well.

4. Place the two turkey breast halves next to each other, ensuring that they are both aligned and matched up like jigsaw puzzle pieces. The skinny end of one breast half should be lined up next to the fatty end of the other breast.

5. Carefully press on the turkey meat to form even cyl-

indrical shapes before tying them with kitchen twine (short length) at 1" intervals. Alternating the ties on every side, begin by tying each end and then continue tying until you have reached the middle.

6. Make sure the turkey meats retain their even cylindrical shapes by adjusting with your hands.

7. Fill a sous vide bag with the tied turkey breasts. Vacuum seal and dry-brine in the refrigerator for up 3 days.

8. Set the sous vide cooker to the target temperature. Remove the dry-brined turkey from the refrigerator and place in the preheated cooker. (You can cook the turkey breasts at 145 degrees for 2 ½ hours.

9. Meanwhile, set the oven temperature at 400 degrees to preheat.

10. Use parchment paper to line a baking sheet (rimmed). Place the turkey skin on the parchment and spread to form a single layer.

11. Be generous with the pepper and salt as you season the laid-out turkey skin. Place another layer of parch-

ment paper on top and then gently press to squeeze any air pockets out.

12. Top the parchment-topped turkey skin with another baking sheet (rimmed) to help keep the turkey skin as it gets cooked.

13. Place the chicken skin in the preheated oven to cook for thirty or forty-five minutes or until really crisp. Once done, remove the skin and allow to cool down to room temperature before storing in a clean container (uncovered) for up to twenty-four hours. In case it turns soft, you can make the turkey skin crisp again by heating in the toaster oven.

14. As soon as the turkey breasts are done, remove the bags from the sous vide cooker. Take the meats out of the bags and then remove all the strings used to tie them. (You may also chill the cooked turkey breasts in the ice bath before storing in the refrigerator for one to seven days. Prior to serving, simply place the chilled turkey breast bags in the preheated water bath (set at 130 degrees) for about one hour.

15. Using even strokes, smoothly slice the turkey meats

with an extremely sharp chef's knife.

16. Place the turkey meat slices on a serving platter (warmed), making sure they form a fanned-out arrangement. Meanwhile, tear the crisp turkey skin into individual portions and place on a serving dish.

17. Serve immediately with homemade gravy and enjoy.

Recipe Using Sous Vide Cooked Extra Crispy-Skinned Turkey:

Easy Turkey Goulash

Ingredients:

- Tomatoes, stewed, diced (14 ounces)

- Tomato sauce (1 cup)

- Basil, dried (1/2 teaspoon)

- Turkey, sous vide cooked, w/ extra crispy skin, cut into one-inch chunks (1 pound)

- Garlic cloves, minced (3 pieces)

- Sugar, white (2 teaspoons)

- Pasta, bow tie (16 ounces)

Directions:

1. Heat a large skillet (nonstick) on medium.

2. Add the turkey chunks and cook until heated through.

3. Add the tomato sauce, stewed tomatoes, basil, sugar, and garlic. Stir to combine, then allow the mixture to simmer for twenty minutes. Once done, remove from heat and set aside.

4. Meanwhile, fill a large pot with water. Add salt and allow to boil. Add the bow tie pasta and cook for about eight to ten minutes or until cooked but still with a firm bite. Once done, drain and transfer into a large bowl.

5. Pour the turkey mixture onto the pasta. Gently toss to combine, making sure the pasta is evenly coated.

6. Serve right away.

16 - Guide to Sous Vide Cooking Pork Chops

Step-by-Step Instructions for Sous Vide Cooking Pork Chops:

1. Place the pork chop on a large plate. Sprinkle on generous amounts of pepper and salt to season it well.

2. Place the seasoned pork chop inside a sous vide bag and vacuum seal. Set aside while you preheat the sous vide cooker.

3. Set the sous vide cooker at 135 to 140 degrees and time for forty-five minutes to four hours of cooking. This ensures that the center will be cooked through without getting too soft.

4. Heat a skillet over medium-high. Add butter and allow it to melt and brown.

5. Once the sous vide cooked pork chop is done, remove from the bag and place it on the skillet. Cook until the meat is seared (but not burned) on all sides. Pay attention to the edges as well as the fat cap, which needs to be rendered to make it crisp and more ap-

petizing.

6. Place the seared pork chop on a plate to cool slightly for about one to two minutes.

7. Serve the seared sous vide pork chop immediately. (Alternatively, you can carve it to separate the fat cap, ribs, and loin from each other. Slice the meat into thin slices and serve right away.)

Recipe Using Sous Vide Cooked Pork Chops:

Apple Cider Pork Chops

Ingredients:

- Salt, kosher (4 tablespoons)

- Butter, unsalted, divided (4 tablespoons)

- Vinegar, apple cider (1/2 teaspoon)

- Black pepper, freshly ground (1/2 teaspoon)

- Thyme leaves, minced, divided (2 teaspoons)

- Parsley, minced (2 teaspoons)

- Pork rib chops, bone in, sous vide cooked, 1-pound (4

pieces)

- Sugar (1 tablespoon)

- Vegetable oil (2 tablespoons)

- Shallot, minced (2 tablespoons)

- Apple cider (3/4 cup)

Directions:

1. Heat a large skillet (cast iron) on medium-high before adding oil. Once heated through, add the butter (1 tablespoon) and allow to melt.

2. Stir in the thyme and shallot; cook for two minutes or until softened.

3. Pour in the apple cider. Stir to combine, reduce heat to medium, and allow the mixture to simmer for four minutes.

4. Add the cider vinegar as well as the remaining butter (3 tablespoons). Whisk well to combine before turning off the heat.

5. Sprinkle salt on the mixture and then stir in the pars-

ley.

6. Pour the prepared apple cider sauce on the sous vide pork chops.

7. Serve and enjoy.

17 - Guide to Sous Vide Cooking Tuna

Step-by-Step Instructions for Sous Vide Cooking Tuna:

1. Generously season all sides of the tuna fillets with pepper and salt.

2. Place the seasoned tuna fillets inside a large sous vide bag. Pour in some extra virgin olive (2 teaspoons for each fillet), gently turning the fillets with your hands so that all sides are evenly coated and kept from sticking to one another.

3. Include parsley/ dill/ thyme, freshly grated citrus zest, thin shallot slices, or other gentle aromatics in the tuna fillet bag. (Make sure not to add any chunky foods to avoid distorting the shape of the tuna. Avoid putting in any acidic foods as well to help retain the texture of the fish.)

4. Vacuum seal the tuna bag and place in the refrigerator overnight. This will help the tuna flesh get firmed up by the salt.

5. Meanwhile, set the sous vide cooker to the target cooking temperature to preheat as the tuna rests and gets dry-brined.

6. Submerge the tuna bag in the preheated sous vide cooker to cook for thirty to forty-five minutes (if cooking 1" thick fillets) or forty-five minutes to one hour (if cooking 2" thick fillets).

7. Once the tuna fillets are done, carefully take out of the sous vide bag and set on a large plate lined with two to three layers of paper towels. Add a layer of paper towel on top and blot gently to dry the surface of the cooked tuna fillets.

8. Remove the aromatics before placing in the refrigerator to chill.

9. Serve right away.

Step-by-Step Instructions for Finishing the Sous Vide Cooked Tuna (Stovetop):

1. Remove the aromatics before seasoning the sous vide cooked tuna fillets. You can sprinkle them with black pepper or roll them in some sesame seeds.

2. Heat a heavy skillet on high before adding oil (1 tablespoon). Allow the oil to get heated through and give off a little smoke before adding the tuna. Cook for about thirty to forty-five seconds. Flip the fish to sear on the other side, then hold sideways with tongs to sear around the edges as well.

3. Place the seared tuna on a plate lined with paper towels to drain off excess oil. Serve as is or sliced, and enjoy.

Recipe Using Sous Vide Cooked Tuna:

Tuna and Peas Orecchiette

Ingredients:

- Orechiette, dried (1 pound)

- Red chili flakes (1 teaspoon)

- Black pepper, freshly ground (1/2 teaspoon)

- Olive oil, extra virgin (1/3 cup)

- Lemon zest, freshly grated (1 tablespoon)

- Lemon juice, freshly squeezed (2 teaspoons)

- Salt, kosher (1/2 teaspoon)

- Peas, frozen (1 cup)

- Garlic clove, peeled, sliced thinly (1 piece)

- Tuna, sous vide cooked with olive oil (5 ounces)

- Parsley leaves, fresh, chopped (1/4 cup)

Directions:

1. Fill a large pot with salted water. Allow it to boil before adding the pasta; cook following the directions indicated on the package.

2. About half a minute before the pasta is al dente, stir the peas into the boiling salted water.

3. Once the pasta and peas are done, drain into a large bowl and set aside. Meanwhile, reserve some of the cooking liquid (about ½ cup).

4. Heat a small skillet over medium before adding olive oil. Once the oil shimmers, stir in the garlic as well as chili flakes. Cook for one minute or until fragrant, then place in a small bowl. Set aside.

5. Place the cooked pasta into a clean pot. Break the sous vide cooked tuna into flaked chunks and add to the pasta. Pour in the chili oil mixture before heating the pot on high.

6. Stir the pasta mixture as you add the reserved pasta liquid (1/2 cup), lemon juice and lemon zest. Continue stirring until the mixture is thickened and the pasta is evenly coated with it.

7. Serve sprinkled with pepper and salt, then topped with parsley.

8. Enjoy.

18 - Guide to Sous Vide Cooking Lobster

Step-by-Step Instructions for Sous Vide Cooking Lobster:

1. Plunge a knife straight into the heads of two live lobsters (whole, each weighing 1½ pounds). Once killed, split each lobster's carapace into halves and twist off their claws and tails.

2. After discarding the carapace, lay the lobster tails flat against a heavy cutting board. Stick 2 skewers (wooden/metal) through the tails; set aside on a large plate.

3. Fill a large pot with water and heat on high. Once boiling, add the lobster tails as well as the claw. Cook the tails for one minute before transferring to an ice bath. Once the tails are cooked after four additional minutes, transfer into the ice bath as well.

4. After shucking the lobster tails, remove the meat and place in a large bowl. Set aside.

5. Crack the shell of the lobster claws to open, then ex-

tract the meat and add to the bowl containing the meat from the lobster tails.

6. Remove the meat from the lobster knuckles and place in the same bowl containing the tail and claw meat.

7. Set the sous vide cooker to the target temperature.

8. Transfer the lobster meat into a sous vide bag. Top with unsalted butter (2 tablespoons) and fresh tarragon sprigs (2 pieces). Vacuum seal and submerge into the sous vide cooker.

9. Allow the lobster meat to cook for twenty minutes to one hour.

10. Once done, remove the bag from the cooker. Take out the lobster meat (minus the tarragon) and set on a platter. Top with hot clarified butter (1/4 cup) and lemon wedges.

11. Serve immediately.

Recipe Using Sous Vide Cooked Lobster:

Mayo Lobster Rolls

Ingredients:

- Lobster, sous vide cooked, completely cooled (2 ½ pounds)

- Mayonnaise, homemade (2 tablespoons)

- Chives, fresh, minced (1/2 tablespoon)

- Tarragon, fresh, minced (1/2 tablespoon)

- Salt, kosher (1/2 teaspoon)

- Black pepper, freshly ground (1/2 teaspoon)

- Butter, unsalted (2 tablespoons)

- Hotdog buns, top split (4 pieces)

- Rib celery, diced finely (1 piece)

- Lemon juice, freshly squeezed (1 tablespoon)

Directions:

1. Heat a large skillet over medium. Add the butter and allow to melt and foam.

2. Add the hot dog buns to the butter, making sure their exposed crumbs sides are facing down. Cook until golden brown before flipping to the other side. After

half a minute, place the hot dog buns on a platter. Set aside.

3. Take the herbs inside the sous vide bag containing the lobster. Transfer the cooked lobster to a plate and chop into one-inch cubes. Place in a large bowl.

4. Add celery, tarragon/ chives, mayonnaise, and lemon juice to the lobster bowl. Gently toss to combine, then season with pepper and salt.

5. Top the hot dog buns with the lobster mixture and serve right away.

19 - Guide to Sous Vide Cooking Carnitas

Step-by-Step Instructions for Sous Vide Cooking Carnitas:

1. Place the pork meat in a large bowl.

2. Add onion (1 piece, roughly chopped), garlic cloves (2 pieces), freshly squeezed orange juice, orange slices (from 1 fruit), bay leaves (2 pieces), and cinnamon stick (1 piece). Toss with the pork, then fold in some salt (1/2 tablespoon) to season the meat well and help it stay moist when cooked.

3. Place the seasoned pork in the sous vide bag. Add the aromatics before vacuum sealing the bag.

4. Set the sous vide cooker at your target temperature to preheat. Drop the pork meat bag into the water bath and allow it to sink. Cook until the meat is tenderly done, then remove from the cooker.

5. Take the sous vide cooked pork out of the bag and place in a large bowl. Discard the aromatics and set the bag juices aside.

6. Use forks to shred the pork meat immediately.

7. Place the shredded pork on a baking sheet (rimmed). Cook under the broiler (preheated), turning the meat occasionally until all sides are crisp and browned. (Alternatively, add the shredded meat to a skillet preheated on medium-high; toss in the pan until crisp on all sides. Or, if you sous vide cooked the pork meat at 145 to 165 degrees, slice into large cubes before cooking in a preheated skillet until browned and seared all over.)

Recipe Using Sous Vide Cooked Carnitas:

Salsa Verde Sous Vide Carnitas

Ingredients:

- Cinnamon stick, cut into 4 portions (1 piece)

- Onion, medium, chopped roughly (1 piece)

- Orange, medium, w/ intact peel (1 piece)

- Salt, kosher (1/2 teaspoon)

- Pork shoulder, boneless, sliced into two-inch-thick

portions (4 pounds)

- Bay leaves (2 pieces)

- Garlic cloves, medium (6 pieces)

Salsa verde:

- Anchovy fillets (6 pieces)

- Mustard (a dollop)

- Basil leaves (a handful)

- Lemon juice, freshly squeezed (1 tablespoon)

- Parsley, flat leaf (a handful)

- Capers (1 tablespoon)

- Garlic clove (1 piece)

- Olive oil, extra virgin (8 tablespoons)

Garnishings:

- Lime wedges

- Salsa verde, charred

- White onion, chopped

- Cilantro leaves, fresh

- Corn tortillas, warm

Directions:

1. Place the pork in a large bowl. Add the cinnamon stick, onion, bay leaves, and garlic.

2. Squeeze the juice out of the orange and into the pork mixture bowl. Add salt and then toss until well-combined.

3. Place the pork mixture into a sous vide bag. Vacuum seal and place in the sous vide cooker to cook to the target time and temperature.

4. Once the pork meat is done, remove from the sous vide bag and place in a large bowl. Transfer any meat chunks onto a baking sheet (rimmed) after discarding the pouch juices and aromatic herbs,

5. Roughly shred the pork meat and then spread at the bottom of the baking sheet. Set aside.

6. Place all ingredients for the salsa verde in a medium bowl. Whisk well to combine; set aside.

7. Meanwhile, set the broiler on high to preheat. Cook the pork under the broiler for about ten minutes or until crisp and nicely browned.

8. Remove the carnitas from the broiler and divide among warm tortillas. Garnish with cilantro/ white onion/ lime wedges.

9. Serve alongside the salsa verde and enjoy.

20 - Guide to Sous Vide Cooking Glazed Vegetables

Step-by-Step Instructions for Sous Vide Cooking Glazed Vegetables:

1. Set the sous vide cooker at 183 degrees to preheat.

2. Scrub one pound of whole baby carrots thoroughly before peeling. Alternatively, you can use one pound of medium or large carrots; chop into one inch cubes after scrubbing and peeling.

3. Fill a sous vide bag with the carrots. Add unsalted butter (2 tablespoons), granulated sugar (1 tablespoon), and kosher salt (1/2 teaspoon).

4. Vacuum seal the carrot bag and then submerge in the preheated water bath. Cook for one hour or until the carrots are completely tender. (If not serving right away, place in the refrigerator; use within one week.)

5. Remove the sous vide cooked carrots out of the bag and transfer onto a large skillet (heavy bottomed). Heat on high and cook, stirring frequently, for two minutes or until the liquid is reduced and glossy.

6. Sprinkle additional kosher salt (1/4 teaspoon) as well as black pepper (1/4 teaspoon) on the carrot mixture. Stir to combine. Add fresh chopped parsley (1 tablespoon) into the mix and stir again. In case the glaze breaks, you can always stir in a little water to bring back the glaze.

7. Serve right away.

8. You can easily replace the carrots, using the same steps, with any of these vegetables:

- Turnips, small, peeled, w/ trimmed stems, chopped into one-inch cubes

- Baby artichokes, trimmed, sliced into quarters

- Radishes, small, scrubbed, w/ trimmed stems

- Onions, small, peeled

- Parsnips, peeled, chopped into one-inch chunks

Recipe Using Sous Vide Cooked Glazed Vegetables:

Deliciously Glazed Carrots

Ingredients:

- Butter (1 tablespoon)

- Sugar, granulated (1/8 teaspoon)

- Nutmeg, ground (1/8 teaspoon)

- Salt, kosher (1/4 teaspoon)

- Black pepper, freshly ground (1/4 teaspoon)

- Baby carrots, Chantenay (1 pound)

- Ginger, ground (1/8 teaspoon)

- Clove, ground (1/8 teaspoon)

- Water, filtered (1/4 cup)

Directions:

1. Fill a large skillet with water.

2. Add the carrots as well as sugar, butter, nutmeg, clove, and ginger. Stir to combine.

3. Cook for about fifteen minutes or until the carrots have tenderized and the glaze has thickened.

4. Stir in pepper and salt.

5. Serve and enjoy.

21 - Guide to Sous Vide Cooking Other Favorite Foods

Step-by-Step Instructions for Sous Vide Cooking Poached Eggs:

1. Place eggs in the preheated water bath to cook to your desired level of tenderness; between 143 and 145 degrees would be great, especially if you cook the eggs for forty-five minutes. (Once the eggs are done, you may let the eggs sit at 130 degrees before serving; you might also place them in the refrigerator to rest overnight.)

2. Take the eggs out of their shells by gently hitting the large ends of the shells on a cutting board or any flat surface. Once cracked, use your right hand's fingertips to carefully remove a tiny part of the peel as you hold an entire egg with your left hand. Doing so will cause the watery egg white (loose) to start dripping out of the shell. Repeat with the rest of the eggs.

3. Place the peeled eggs in a large bowl. Do this gently so that what comes out of each shell is a smooth-edged, soft, gelled egg white with the egg yolk intact

inside. Make sure any loose egg white portions are left in the shells (you can do this by carefully spooning out the eggs prior to dumping out the loose egg white parts).

4. Meanwhile, heat a pot filled with water on medium-high and allow to boil. Once boiling, reduce heat to low and wait for the water to barely simmer. Add the peeled eggs at this point and allow them to start setting around their edges.

5. Keep the eggs from sticking to the pot as well as becoming distended to one side by swirling the simmering water from time to time. Let the eggs develop skins by cooking them for about one minute.

6. Once done, carefully spoon out the eggs from the pot. They should come out having a perfect oval shape, an opaque white color, and a delicate skin on the outside.

7. If not serving right away, transfer the poached eggs into a prepared ice bath, then place in the refrigerator to keep for one to two days.

8. Before serving, drop the poached eggs into a water bath set at 130 to 140 degrees for about ten minutes.

Step-by-Step Instructions for Sous Vide Cooking Soft-Boiled Eggs:

1. Cook the eggs as you normally would a 3-minute egg: Heat a pot filled with water until boiling; carefully drop in the eggs and let them sit for three minutes, and transfer them into an ice bath.

2. Meanwhile, set the sous vide cooker at 143 degrees to preheat.

3. After one minute in the ice bath, remove the eggs and submerge in the preheated water bath. Allow them to cook for forty-five minutes.

4. Peel the sous vide soft-boiled eggs as you would a regular soft-boiled egg.

Step-by-Step Instructions for Sous Vide Cooking Bacon:

1. Set the sous vide cooker at 145 degrees.

2. Fill a sous vide bag with the bacon (1 pound, thick-cut) OR leave the bacon in its original plastic container. Submerge in the sous vide cooker to cook for eight to forty-eight hours.

3. Once done, take the bacon out of the water bath and place in the refrigerator to chill, store in the freezer for using later, or serve immediately.

4. Finish your sous vide bacon by first heating a large skillet for five minutes on medium-high. Add the bacon and let cook on one side for two minutes or until crisp and browned. Flip the bacon to cook on the other side for about fifteen seconds or until no longer pale.

5. Place the bacon pieces on a plate lined with paper towels. Allow any excess fat drain off before serving.

Step-by-Step Instructions for Sous Vide Cooking Breakfast Ham:

1. Set the sous vide cooker at 145 degrees to preheat.

2. Meanwhile, fill a sous vide bag with breakfast ham (8

slices, stacked/separated).

3. Drop the ham-filled bag into the preheated water bath. Cook for six to twelve hours.

4. Once the sous vide ham is done, place in the refrigerator and use within one week, store in the freezer and use within three months (before finishing and serving, thaw in the refrigerator overnight first), or serve right away.

   Heat a large skillet (cast iron/ stainless steel) on medium-high. Add vegetable oil (1 tablespoon) and allow to shimmer and get heated through. Add the sous vide ham and cook for about two minutes or until crisp and nicely seared on just one side. Place on a warm platter, serve and enjoy.

Thank You

As we reach the end of this book, I want to say thanks for reading this book.

I want to get this information out to as many people as possible. If you found this book helpful, I would greatly appreciate you leaving me a review. This helps others find the book as well.

Disclaimer

This document is geared towards providing exact and reliable information in regards to the topic and issue covered. The publication is sold on the idea that the publisher is not required to render an accounting, officially permitted, or otherwise, qualified services. If advice is necessary, legal, financial, medical or professional, a practiced individual in the profession should be ordered.

This information is not presented by a financial or medical practitioner and is for entertainment, educational and informational purposes only. The content is not intended as a substitute for professional medical advice, diagnosis, or treatment. Always seek the advice of your physician or other qualified health care provider with any questions you may have regarding a medical condition. Never disregard professional medical advice or delay in seeking it because of something you have read.

The information provided herein is stated to be truthful and consistent, in that any liability, in terms of inattention or otherwise, by any usage or abuse of any policies, processes, or directions contained within is the solitary and utter responsibility of the recipient reader. Under no circumstances will any legal responsibility or blame be held against the

DISCLAIMER

publisher for any reparation, damages, or monetary loss due to the information herein, either directly or indirectly.

Last Updated: 07.Dec.2017